The War Chronicles of Jerzy Dobiecki

By
Ian von Heintze

Front Cover
Painting by **B. Slezkin** – Poland 1978, oil on canvas:
Mounted officer of the 18th Polish Pomeranian Lancers Regiment

Image of regimental cross reproduced by kind permission of **Sławomir Ziętarski,**
(18th Polish Pomeranian Lancers Regimental Volunteer Association, Poland)
Photograph: **Jerzy Dobiecki**, Rotmistrz (Cavalry Captain), 18th Polish Pomeranian
Lancers Regiment, whilst on attachment to the Ministry of Military Affairs, Poland
1939

(Elsewhere in this book, unless otherwise indicated, photographs and images have
been selected from the author's own collection)

The War Chronicles of Jerzy Dobiecki by Ian von Heintze
Cover painting by B. Slezkin
This edition published in 2018

Winged Hussar Publishing is an imprint of

Pike and Powder Publishing Group LLC
17 Paddock Drive   1525 Hulse Rd, Unit 1
Lawrence, NJ 08648   Point Pleasant, NJ 08742

Copyright © Ian von Heintze
ISBN 978-1-945430-73-2
LCN 2018952376

Bibliographical References and Index
1. History. 2. Poland. 3. World War II

Pike and Powder Publishing Group LLC All rights reserved
For more information on Pike and Powder Publishing Group, LLC,
visit us at www.PikeandPowder.com & www.wingedhussarpublishing.com

twitter: @pike_powder
facebook: @PikeandPowder
facebook: Winged Hussar Publishing

By the same author:

'To Remain on File'

For

Jerzy Stanisław DOBIECKI
(My Grandfather)

CONTENTS

Ian von Heintze

HELP WITH PRONUNCIATION OF POLISH WORDS[1]

The Polish Alphabet:

a b c d e f g h i j k l m n o p r s t u w y z
ą ć ę   ł   ń ó   ś   ż
                                    ź

(No 'q', 'v' or 'x' as in English)

Sound of the vowels in Polish:
a – as in h**al**f or l**au**gh
ą – as in **own** without quite finishing the n
e – as in t**e**n
ę – as in m**en**
i – as in h**ea**t or s**ea**t
o – as in N**o**vember
ó – sounds like 'oo' in l**oo**k hence Krak**ó**w becomes 'Krak**oof**'
u – as in b**oo**k
y – as in s**i**t

Sound of consonants in Polish:

c –	sounds like 'ts' as in f**its**
ć –	sounds like ch in scree**ch**
cz –	sounds like 'ch' in **ch**ur**ch** or **ch**oose
chrz –	sounds like lo**ch sh**ore
dż –	sounds like 'j' as in **j**ewel or **j**ungle
g –	sounds always like **g**ive (not like **g**eometry)
grz –	sounds like lu**xur**ious
j –	sounds like 'y' in **y**east
krz –	sounds like too**k s**ugar
ł –	sounds like 'w' in **w**et
ń –	sounds like soft 'n' as in Spanish 'ma**ñ**ana'
prz –	sounds like sto**p sh**outing
rz –	sounds like 's' as in plea**s**ure
sz and **ż** –	sound like 's' in mea**s**ure or trea**s**ure
trz –	sounds like mu**ch s**ugar
w –	sounds like 'v' or 'f'

b, d, f, h, k, l, m, n, p, r, s, t and **z** are pronounced more or less as in English

FOREWORD

As I write this note, the Great War has been over for more than one hundred years. The Second World War, a little more recently, ended seventy-three years ago. Arguably one of the greatest generations in history will, in the not too distant future, no longer be able to provide us with its first-hand accounts of what it meant to live through these most devastating of conflicts.

Despite facing impossible odds, the men and women who fought for Poland between 1939 and 1945, were forced to take the fight to the enemy as exiles from their own country, becoming the fourth largest combatitive nationality to represent the Allied forces in the struggle against Naziism. Despite Poland's officer corps being virtually decimated at Katyn by those who were supposedly on the same side, and notwithstanding the exclusion of Polish troops from the victory parades on the streets of London following the end of the war, Poland has remained a steadfast and loyal ally. Indeed, Poland's overall contribution to the Second World War has often been downplayed and only over time has a more honest and rounded appraisal of Poland's impact upon this period begun to emerge.

One of the reasons that this has been possible, has been the gradual shedding of light on the facts, often underpinned by the testimony of individuals who witnessed events first-hand. Today, the continuing acknowledgement of what was achieved by that generation, is one of the ways that we might continue to honour the individual sacrifices made. Ian von Heintze has gone some way to pay tribute to the Poles who lived through the two world wars and to his grandfather in particular, whose eye-witness accounts of events during this period need to be told.

I am sure there are many more reports, like Jerzy's that still remain to be aired and with each revelation, thankfully, we take a further step nearer to immortalizing the truth.

Vincent Rospond
New Jersey
November 2018

AUTHOR'S NOTE

Since the end of hostilities of the Great War that had lasted from 1914 to 1918, many of the place-names that were written about by my grandfather in his early chronicles, today unfortunately either no longer exist or have at the very least acquired variations in spelling over time. By way of example, the city of **Daugavpils** in present-day Latvia, was known as *Dyneburg* in 1920 (and referred-to as such in Jerzy's account of his regiment's engagements there); At different times it has also been called *Dūnaburg, Borisoglebsk, Dvinsk* and *Dźwińsk*. Similarly, *Horodyszcze* in Belarus is today spelt *Haradzišča*; **Iszkołdź** (Belarus) is now *Iškaldź*; **Vilnius** (Lithuania) and **L'viv** (today in the Ukraine) when formerly part of Poland, were called *Wilno* and *Lwów* respectively. *Memel*, formerly part of Eastern Prussia, is today **Klaipeda** in Lithuania. *Danzig*, Poland's principle port on the Baltic sea, is now more widely known as **Gdańsk**. In some instances, particularly since the early nineteenth century, the names of settlements, rural communities, small towns and villages located in the parts of Poland and eastern Europe about which my grandfather wrote whilst deployed with a fledgling Polish army between 1919 and 1921, may have disappeared from maps altogether. As a consequence, there are many locations that were mentioned in *Jerzy's* journals that unfortunately do not appear on any of the maps that feature in this book. The names of places that he mentions in his accounts have been shown as he noted them and if contemporarily known by another name or if they are spelled differently today, the present spelling is displayed in brackets.

In order to assist the reader, the convention used throughout this book is to show Austrian, German/Prussian, Polish, Lithuanian, Latvian, Belorussian, Ukrainian and Russian place names, as well as all Polish, French and Eastern European proper names, in italics. If a place, village, town or city that is mentioned in the text has been identified on any one of the maps included in this book, then the place name has been highlighted in **bold** in the body of the text.

PREFACE

This story of my grandfather's life – between 1895 and 1958, is based upon English translations of three pieces of work originally written in Polish. The first work used in this book is a short history about his regiment – the 18th Polish Pomeranian Lancers (in Polish, '*18-ty Pułk Ułanów Pomorskich*'). This historical account was written by *Jerzy* whilst serving in the rank of lieutenant, together with Captain *Michał Kłopotowski* of the same regiment, and was published in 1929 in Poland as part of a larger body of work about the history of Poland's cavalry and other military formations. My grandfather's publication provides a rare eye-witness account of the 18th Pomeranian Lancers' operations during the 1919-1921 Russo-Polish War[1] – a conflict that has since received comparatively little notoriety in English[2] despite the significance of the outcome of this war at the time for the rest of Europe. (It was during this campaign that the Polish army played a big part in stalling the momentum behind Russia's efforts to roll out communist ideology westwards towards the rest of Europe, following the end of the Great War). Although the 18th Pomeranian Lancers were not operationally engaged in the more widely reported battle for **Warsaw** in August of 1920 – considered perhaps to be one of the pivotal moments of the Russo-Polish War, *Jerzy* and his regiment were deployed a few weeks later, in September 1920 during the subsequent Polish offensive at the Battle of **Niemen** (neighboring present-day Belarus) to decisively push back the Russian army.

As an aside, historians have gone as far as to suggest that after **Warsaw** was prevented from falling to the Russian army in 1920, the subsequent battle between Polish and Russian cavalry near **Zamość**[3] in south-east Poland, could most probably be regarded as the last, notable, cavalry battle in European history.

The second translation upon which this book has been based, is a brief history of the every-day regimental routine of 18th Polish Pomeranian Lancers and is a piece written more recently in Polish by *Sławomir Ziętarski*, for the 18th Polish Pomeranian Lancers Regimental Volunteer Association in Poland. This organization today commemorates and continues the traditions of this former Polish cavalry regiment that was dissolved in 1939 and was not later resurrected as part of Poland's new modern-day army, following the end of the Second World War.

The third work used in this book, is the English translation of my grandfather's personal log. In 1939, during the first weeks of the Second World War and whilst posted away from his regiment on secondment to Poland's military high command in **Warsaw**, *Jerzy* was once again writing about events in Poland, contemporaneously recording in a diary, details of the Polish military deployments and battles fought across Poland as German troops advanced eastwards during September and the first weeks of October of that year. When Russian forces unexpectedly crossed into Poland from the east on 17 September 1939, this made it impossible for the Poles to defend an onslaught on two fronts. Having already steadily retreated across Poland with the military leadership in the face of the overwhelming German attack, my grandfather received orders to evacuate to neighboring Romania, together with elements of the army's headquarters staff, many other Polish soldiers and with officials of the Polish government. Later In 1940, *Jerzy* submitted sections of this diary as part of a formal military deposition,[4] in response to orders by one of the several Commissions of Enquiry[5] set-up by the, then exiled, Polish Government in France; these Commissions had been established to identify the causes of Poland's rapid capitulation in 1939[6], during what had become known as the 'Polish September Campaign'.

The translations of *Jerzy's* jointly published chronicle of the 18th Polish Pomeranian Lancers' campaigns during the Russo-Polish War, together with the history of the regiment written more recently by Mr *Ziętarski* (providing a brief picture of the regiment's history from 1919 until its dissolution in 1939), have been joined together and form the basis of chapters 4 to 6 of this book and are used as the backdrop to what little is known about my grandfather's life during this period. *Jerzy's* diary of the Second World War appears as a translation into English in chapter 8.

Jerzy Dobiecki lived through an extraordinary period of Poland's history. In the course of his lifetime he was actively engaged in three wars. As a professional soldier, he found himself wearing, at one time or another, the uniform or insignia of four different armies – that of the Imperial Russian Army from 1915 to 1918, the badges of two different regiments of the Independent Polish Army between 1919 and 1939, later the uniform of the Free Polish Army in exile from 1940 to 1945, and eventually held the rank of Captain as a member of the Polish Resettlement Corps – part of the British Army, between 1946 and 1948.

Jerzy was born in eastern Poland, at a time when that part of the country was under Tsarist Russian control and Poland was recovering from efforts by three neighboring empires to have her removed, one hundred years previously, from the political map of Europe.[7] My grandfather would spend twenty of his thirty-two-year military career as a cavalry officer with the 18th Polish Pomeranian Lancers – performing operational, training and administrative roles. In 1914, as Europe was plunged into the fighting of the Great War, *Jerzy* was nineteen years old; 'Poland' as we know it today simply did not exist. All that we now regard as Poland was controlled by three neighboring empires, the Great Powers of Europe – Russia, Austria-Hungary and Prussia (Germany). *Jerzy's* life as a soldier began as a volunteer in the Russian Imperial Army in 1915. On return from duty at the Eastern Front of the Great War three years later, he enlisted with the fledgling Polish Army that had just been formed following Poland's acquisition of independence after the end of hostilities in 1918. Within months and following initial officer cadet training, *Jerzy* was attached to a newly formed regiment of the renowned Polish cavalry. This was to take him straight back to the front-line in one of the six wars then being fought between Poland and her neighbors – conflicts that arose as a consequence of the way territory had been partitioned in Eastern Europe during the post-war settlement of 1919.

In order to give a historical context to *Jerzy's* chronicles and a brief insight to some of Poland's history of this period to those who may not be familiar with it, Appendix One of this book provides a brief timeline of some of the events that occurred in this part of Europe between 1795 (when a free Poland had been dealt a severe blow as the country was swallowed up by its neighbors[8]), up to the rebirth of Poland as an independent sovereign nation following the fall of communism later in 1989. In drawing-together these specific moments in the country's history, an attempt has been made to show some of the historical milestones that had shaped Poland before 1895 – when Jerzy was born, and the changes that occurred subsequently during the sixty-three years of his life, up to 1958. Poland continued to see monumental transformation during this period. If, for instance, a Pole travelled from **Warsaw** to **Poznań** in the 1820s, (both located in Poland today) they would have crossed into a different country.[9] The transformations of Poland's identity as a state would continue into the 20th and 21st Centuries; between 1916 and 2016 Poland has had no fewer than twenty-nine Heads of State and in the same period, over fifty Prime Ministers – not including those nominated to lead the government that had been established (on more than one occasion) in exile. The country's name has changed at least seven times and her borders – that feature on a map of Central Europe today, bear no resemblance to those of, say, 1795, 1809, 1815 or 1939.

I think you will become quickly familiar with my grandfather's story. It is so similar to that told by the many other Poles who, at the end of the Second World War in 1945 for example, after fighting alongside the allies to liberate Europe, had no home of their own left to return-to in Poland. Many had to make a choice between either a life in exile – in a country that some felt had enough problems of its own recovering from the war, or a return to Poland – by then behind the Iron Curtain and in the grip of communism, and to try to become involved in the effort to rebuild their lives there, despite the very real threat of harassment, persecution, prosecution and even death as potential 'enemies of the state'.

As I write this book and reflect upon the many conversations that I had with my grandmother, my parents, my (Great) uncles and aunts – all Poles, and each one of whom left Poland in various guises as a result of the Second World War to initially settle in Britain or France, it seems to me that perhaps what haunted them most were not their recollections of the war, but the total and abject dread of the brutality that they might have faced in Poland were they to have remained there at the time of the post-war severities imposed by the Stalinist regime. This book hopefully sheds some light on how the circumstances in Europe in 1945 and in Britain in particular, impacted upon and shaped some of my grandfather's decisions as he contemplated a future once the war was over, both for himself and for his immediate family.

Ian von Heintze

POLISH CAVALRY LEGEND

In the previous section I alluded very briefly to the traditionally-held high esteem of Poland's cavalry. The prowess of such units around the world as the Knights Templar, the Teutonic Knights, the Mongol warriors, the Russian Cossacks, the Persian Aswarans, the Ottoman Sipahi, the Japanese Samurai, Roman cavalry, native American Indians, Egyptian Mamluks and the Polish Winged Hussars for example, are well catalogued. Often, the cavalry units became the elite regiments of a nation's army or principal fighting force.

Through the Ages, as methods, techniques and approaches to warfare evolved, so too did the effectiveness and the choice of deployment in battle of the mounted soldier. In ancient times, the use of the horseman (cavalryman) was seen as an additional tactic in battle, to be used in support of the deployment of massed soldiers on foot (the infantry). With the development of military philosophy, weaponry, strategy, technology and equipment the cavalryman's function became more dominant in battle and at the same time dependent upon his precise role, the size of his horse and how much armor or other equipment he was expected to carry. In earlier times, a unit of cavalry might have been divided between horse archers, light cavalry and heavy cavalry. The 'mass cavalry' formation in battle progressively became a more important force in medieval military doctrine. Later, in western European tactics it was adopted as the main striking force for nearly all armies on the European battlefield, prior to the eventual introduction of missile-firing weapons – such as muskets and cannon, when the cavalry's role was reviewed.

In the Polish-Lithuanian Commonwealth of the 15th Century, units of cavalry were described as 'Lancer' regiments (*Ułanów* in Polish) so named after the lance that was issued as the primary strike weapon – a four to six-meter length of hollowed pole made of fir-wood, with a forged steel tip and a pennon or regimental flag attached below the tip. This weapon and sometimes an even longer version were carried later in the 16th and 17th centuries by the heavier, armored cavalry known as 'Hussars' (or Husaria) who were additionally equipped with a sword, a sabre (and usually bow with arrows as well), and whose primary combat tactic during battle was the charge.

Although historians are not universally in agreement about the source of the word, *'Hussar'* is commonly held to be Hungarian in origin and used to describe a heavily armed cavalryman. Mounted units of Hussars were first formed in the Polish/Lithuanian Commonwealth using Serbian mercenaries who had crossed into Poland from Hungary during the 15th century. As these Polish regiments of Hussars evolved they would later become famous and readily identifiable for the huge wings that each cavalryman had on his back or attached to his saddle – ostensibly a wooden frame sprouting eagle, ostrich, swan or goose feathers – often secured to the rider's armor-plate. Among the numerous theories (see below) that explain their use is the suggestion that these 'wings' made a clattering sound as the cavalryman moved forward at speed and it is believed this would frighten the horses of the enemy or make it sound like the numbers charging the adversary were greater than they actually were. If nothing else, they were a visual distraction of movement. The Polish-Lithuanian Commonwealth fought a number of wars against Swedish, Russian and Turkish armies. The 16th and 17th Centuries saw the height of the fame of the Polish Winged Hussars – notably at the Battle of *Vienna* in 1683.

With the development of gun powder, it became more effective to equip and to train the infantry in the use of muskets, and although massed cavalry charges would retain their place on the battlefield, between the 17th and 19th Centuries, cavalry would increasingly discard their heavy armor to favor greater freedom of movement during combat. There was a resurgence in the use of the lance in the aftermath of the Napoleonic Wars due to the prowess of the Polish lancers (Chevau-Léger-Lancier).

In the years that followed, the weaponry that became available to the cavalryman almost made the lance obsolete and in the interests of costs and efficiency many regiments were gradually dismounted and incorporated into infantry or were eventually mechanized. Nonetheless, mounted troops would play a major part during The Great War of 1914-1918 and remained a conspicuous element of all major European armies following the armistice. Cavalry was used extensively by both sides during the Russo-Polish War from 1919 to 1920.

In 1939, at the outbreak of the Second World War, although units of cavalry were still being maintained, the most significant mounted action took place during the Polish, Balkan and Soviet campaigns of that war. Mounted sections of the 18th Polish Pomeranian Lancers famously became entangled with German mechanized units at **Krojanty** in the north-west of Poland in the afternoon of 1st September 1939 (described later).

One of the last battles of the war during which cavalry was used by both sides, took place in Poland near **Zamość** on 23 September 1939 in the vicinity of the town of *Krasnobród*. Units of the 25th Wielkopolska Ułan Regiment were pitched against forces of the 8th German Infantry Division.

Perhaps one of the very last, confirmed cavalry charges of the Second World War and amongst the last mounted charges in the history of the Polish cavalry, occurred on 1 March 1945 at Żeńsko in the northern Polish region of Pomerania. It involved units of the 1st Independent Warsaw Cavalry Brigade and the 163rd German Infantry Division.

The 18th Polish Pomeranian Lancers, my grandfather's regiment, were decimated during the German attack on Poland in September 1939. The regiment was not resurrected after the war.

In his work about the thousand-year history of the Poles (*"The Polish Way"*), *Adam Zamoyski* mentions the Polish cavalry of the 16th Century, and of the Winged Hussars in particular; I am grateful to Murray Press, an imprint of Hodder & Stoughton, for authority to reproduce the following extract[1]:

"...Cavalry made up the backbone of the Commonwealth's military power and outnumbered the infantry by about three to one. The Poles crossed horses from Turkey with a number of European breeds, without any apparent method but with an instinct for speed and endurance. They rode on eastern saddles, which place less strain on the horse. These two factors explain their ability to cover tremendous distances (up to 120 kilometers a day for several days) without killing their mounts. Their ability to fight for long hours without exhausting themselves stemmed from the fact that their sabre was probably the finest cutting weapon ever in use in a European army. It was the curved eastern sabre, modified by the Hungarians and further adapted by the Poles in the sixteenth century until it reached a combination of length, weight and curve which gave it a uniquely high ratio of cutting-power to effort expended.

The pride and glory of the Polish cavalry, its mailed fist, was the Husaria, the winged cavalry. This operated in regiments of about three hundred men highly skilled and armed to the teeth. The companions of the front rank carried an astonishing lance of up to twenty feet in length, which outreached infantry pikes, allowing the Husaria to cut straight through a square. Having planted his lance in the chest of an enemy pike-man, the companion then drew either his sabre or another weapon peculiar to the Poles, the rapier with a six-foot blade which doubled as a short lance. Each companion also carried a pair of pistols, a short carbine, a bow and arrows and a variety of other weapons – the most lethal of which was the *czekan* – a long steel hammer which could go through heads and helmets like butter. The retainers carried much the same arsenal without the long lance, while the rear rank often led spare mounts into the charge. The bow they carried was the small, curved eastern type, more quick-firing than any musket, accurate at longer ranges and easier to fire from a moving horse.

The Husaria wore helmets, thick steel breastplates and shoulder and arm-guards, or eastern scale armor. The companions also wore wooden arcs bristling with eagle feathers rising over their heads like two wings from attachments on the back of the saddle or the shoulders. Over one shoulder they wore the skin of a tiger or leopard as a cloak. These served to frighten the enemy's horses, and indeed the enemy himself, and the wings had the added advantage of preventing Tatars eager for ransom from lassoing the Polish riders in a mêlée. But the main purpose of these accoutrements was to give an impression of splendor. The companions in the Husaria were young noblemen who liked to show off their wealth. Helmets and breastplates were chased or studded with gold and often set with semi-precious stones. Harnesses, saddles and horse-cloths were embroidered and embellished with gold and gems. The long lance was painted like a stick of rock and decorated with a five-foot-long silk pennant which made a frightful noise at the charge.

For over a century, the Husaria were the lords of the battlefield, *Kircholm* (1605), where 4,000 Poles under Chodkiewicz accounted for 14,000 Swedes, was little more than one long cavalry maneuver ending in the Husaria's charge. *Klushino* (1610), where Żółkiewski with 6,000 Poles, of whom only 200 were infantry, defeated 30,000 Muscovites and 5,000 German and Scottish mercenaries, was a Husaria victory, as was the battle of *Gniew* (1656), in which 5,500 Polish cavalry defeated 13,000 Swedes. In many other battles, from *Byczyna* (1588) and *Trzciana* (1629) to the relief of *Vienna* (1683), the Husaria dealt the decisive blow......"

One can only imagine whether or to what extent a desire to follow in the tradition of the Hussar may have played a part in motivating my grandfather to enlist in 1919 for cavalry training. What he could not have known at the time, was that one day he would become a staff officer with the command of the Polish 1st Corps – formed in exile in Britain during World War II, a Division of which would have as its emblem, the Polish Winged Hussars' distinctive helmet and legendary wings (see image in photograph section of chapter 8, Gen. Montgomery shaking hands with Polish soldiers). Both *Jerzy's* brother and future son-in-law (my father) would also later serve with regiments of this division of the Polish army in exile – the 1st Polish Armored Division.

Panoply with elaborate frame of bird feathers – Armor of the Polish 'Winged' Hussars – Poland's cavalry during the 16th/17th Century (The armor shown was formerly on display at the British War Museum, London and is part of a private collection) Image reproduced by kind permission of Nigel Carren (www.nigelcarren.co.uk) ©Nigel Carren

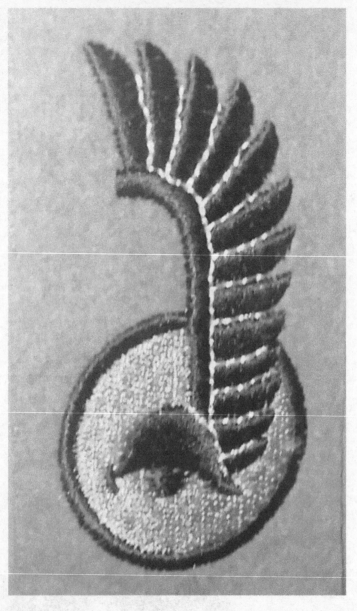

Replica arm-patch of that worn by soldiers of the 1st Polish Armored Division, formed in Britain during February 1942. (The emblem depicts the wings and armored helmet of the Polish Husaria during the 16th & 17th Centuries)

Ian von Heintze
CHAPTER 1
EARLY YEARS
(1895 – 1914)

Jerzy Stanisław Dobiecki was born a Pole, on 24th January 1895 in *Poturzyn* which, at the end of the 19th century was a small village located in the county of *Tomaszów* within the *'Gubernia' Łomżyńska* ('Governorate' of *Łomża*), one of Tsarist Russia's western-most governorates and part of what was known then as the Russian *'Vistula Province'* (or in Russian, *'Privislinskiy kray'*). The name 'Poland' had been removed from any maps or official documents in circulation during previous years of the russification of eastern Poland, since roughly the 1830's and following the Partitions of Poland between neighboring empires at the end of the 18th Century. The former 'Kingdom of Poland' was largely abolished in 1864 and the administrative structures in those parts of Poland that fell under Russian rule, were progressively dismantled and drawn into line with the local government model of the rest of the Russian Empire. This empire at the time covered some 8 million square miles and the Russian Tsar had jurisdiction over approximately 170 million people. The crowned eagle – the national emblem of the Poles – became obsolete. The use of the Polish language in official matters was replaced by Russian in the part of Poland where *Jerzy* was born.

Today, one hundred and twenty years later, **Poturzyn** (see map Appendix Two), lies in the commune of *Telatyn* in south-eastern Poland, literally a stone's-throw away from the Polish-Ukrainian border and part of the *'Województwo Lubelskie'* – the Province of *Lublin* (the country's former provincial administrative structure having been restored throughout Poland in 1999).

Jerzy was born on the family estate (also called 'Poturzyn') that belonged to his grandparents – *Kazimierz Dobiecki* and *Natalia Rulikowska* (see family tree at Appendix Three), and was the eldest of four children, all of whom were born in their grandparents' house. His younger brother, *Kazimierz ('Kazio')* was born a year later in 1896, his sister *Janina ('Jania')* in 1898 and youngest brother *Stanisław ('Stach')* was born eight years after that, in 1906.

Jerzy was born into a Polish family that had enjoyed, the recognition and status of landed-gentry since the eighteenth century. His grandfather, *Kazimierz Józef Bonifacy Dobiecki*, a *Tomaszów* District Judge, had established in 1867 – by way of a decree issued by the state authorities of the former Kingdom of Poland (a document that has withstood the tests of time and still exists today), that Kazimierz's ancestors had been previously granted noble status in 1776 by *Stanisław August Poniatowski*, King of Poland Grand Duke of

Lithuania. This privilege carried with it a hereditary entitlement to bear one of Poland's coats of arms – designated by the heraldic crest known as '*Osoria*' (see Appendix Three). These coats of arms were not personal to the bearers and were borne by all members of the family, and often even by several families of different names.

Stefan Josef Anzelm Dobiecki (*Jerzy's* father), owned and managed one of Poland's first sugar refineries, built in Poturzyn by *Tytus Wojciechowski* (1808-1879), the latter an agriculturalist, political activist and close friend of, amongst others, *Fryderyk Chopin*. *Jerzy*, his parents, brother and sister would spend the winters on *Jerzy's* grandparents' estate in **Poturzyn**, as it was located only a short distance from the sugar processing plant. The factory and accompanying estates had been previously acquired by the *Rulikowski* family (*Jerzy's* grandparents, see family tree at Appendix Three).

In hand-written correspondence that he leaves behind as part of his memoires, Jerzy wrote of the time when he was with his mother, *Konstancja* (formerly *Wiercieńska*)[1] and in 1899, aged about four, he watched a fire at this sugar refinery. He apparently witnessed the fire from the windows of the manor house belonging to family friends – whom he knew as *Pani* (or 'Mrs' in English) *Wydżdżyna* (formerly *Wojciechowska*) and where, as small children, they were often taken to play.

As one might expect following the devastation of the two world wars, very little remains today of some of the homes, buildings and outhouses that were dotted around this rural village at the time that *Jerzy* grew up. Amongst some of the notable relics of the past that are still visible in **Poturzyn** today are the overgrown, red-brick cornerstones that once formed part of the foundations of the sugar refinery, destroyed later during the Second World war, and a small plaque under a tree close to the park commemorating a visit to **Poturzyn** by *Fryderyk Chopin* in 1830.

Returning to *Jerzy's* early childhood, in the non-winter months *Jerzy*, his parents and brothers and sister lived at their main home – a rural manor house belonging to his parents, approximately 6 kilometers to the west of **Poturzyn**, at nearby **Radostów** located to the south-east of **Zamość** in eastern Poland. During the first half of the 19th century, the **Radostów** estate with its 120,000 acres had originally also belonged to the *Rulikowski* family. In 1857, when *Natalia Rulikowska* was married to *Kazimierz Dobiecki* (*Jerzy's* grandfather), the entire estate together with an apartment in **Warsaw**, were given to *Kazimierz Dobiecki* as part of the dowry; thereafter, the property remained in the *Dobiecki* family until both the estates at **Radostów** and **Poturzyn** were later confiscated by the communist Polish government in 1945.

The manor house at **Radostów** and substantial annex (affectionately known by the family as the "rządcówka") at one time opened onto a large lawn and elaborate flower garden set in the center. *Jerzy's* daughter, *Anna* (*"Anita"*), recalls that the lawn was surrounded by a driveway that enabled horses and carriages to be brought up to the front door of the main house. The family owned a number of horses, about twenty in all – some for working in the fields, some for riding and others used for drawing carriages. Other animals on the estate included a menagerie of cows, pigs, chickens and rabbits. The house was patrolled at night by a watchman with dogs, the latter living in kennels and never being allowed into the house. Although only about five years old at the time, Anita is unable to forget the very formal dining arrangements at Radostów; although the family took their meals at the same time, the children were always seated at their own table with '*Pani Helena*', the governess, and no talking was allowed. The adults dined at an adjacent table.

Jerzy wrote a brief note recalling the time when his grandfather, *Kazimierz Dobiecki*, passed away in 1903. *Jerzy's* parents, *Stefan* and *Konstancja*, took *Jerzy* to the funeral and he has a vague recollection of his stay at his grandfather's apartment at 5, Warecka Street in the *Mokotów* district of **Warsaw.**

Depending where in Poland one lived, much of Poland's education system at this time was subject, in varying degrees, to the regulation, administrative systems and bureaucracies of the three occupying empires. In the eastern part of Poland that had been annexed by Russia, all teaching in schools had been in Russian since 1885, and *Jerzy* would have been forbidden to talk with fellow pupils in anything but Russian whilst on the school grounds. Jerzy went to school in **Lublin** between 1910 and 1914, and his military record today shows that besides fluency in Polish, he had a very good command of French (which he was taught at home) and both Russian and German. At some point in his youth, he learned to play the piano and by the time he had reached his teens, had become both a skilled and accomplished horse-rider.

Almost every aspect of *Jerzy's* early life in the farther reaches of rural, eastern Poland would have been impacted-upon by the social, political, cultural, judicial and administrative systems imposed on that part of Poland, following partition of the territory by Russia.   The circumstances in which Poles were living under partition in other parts of Poland at the time varied according to which regime they fell under, as another third of the country was subject to the different rules of the Austro-Hungarian empire and the final third of Poland had been partitioned by Prussia - where the Germanization of the Poles living within that territory, was particularly harsh.

Whilst in his teens and still a full-time student, Jerzy might probably have been aware of events that were unfolding at the time beyond Poland. The unsettled nature of the politics in the Balkans during the period following the collapse of the Turkish empire and the antagonism and suspicion that was growing between Russia, Germany and Austria-Hungary over territorial gains in Europe, may all have been frequent topics of discussion. August 1914 saw the distribution by the press department of the Russian Ministry of Foreign Affairs, of propaganda leaflets throughout Russian Poland. Apart from this and other sources of information that might have been available (general hearsay and gossip, news from those in the know who might have visited the house, official propaganda circulated at school and in the work place, and from information gleaned from posters on general public display), one has to assume that *Jerzy* and his family had access to newspapers, periodicals and journals that gave at least some indication or assessment of the events of the day and an idea of what was happening in Russian Poland and further afield. Despite Russian being the official language of the organs of state in Russian Poland and an increased level of state censorship compared to that experienced within the Austrian zone of occupation, there were nonetheless a number of newspapers and periodicals published in Polish. In the years that led up to 1914 (particularly after 1905) a variety of views were expressed in the newspapers in circulation concerning the turmoil in the Balkans for instance. At the time of the assassination of the heir to the Austrian throne in Sarajevo in 1914, the story was widely reported in Russian Poland and some newspapers even ran special supplements to their usual editions in order to cover the story.

One of the few remaining photographs of the sugar refinery owned and operated by *Jerzy's* grandparents in *Poturzyn*, south-east Poland, prior to its later destruction by fire during World War II *Poturzyn* c1890s

Jerzy's mother, Konstancja Regina Dobiecka (née Wiercieńska) Poland c1890

Jerzy's father, *Stefan Dobiecki*
Poland c1890

Identity card issued in 1880 to *Stefan Dobiecki, Jerzy's* father, confirming his residential status in *Warsaw*.

(The printed words on the document are in Polish although the words entered by hand are written using the Russian Cyrillic alphabet)

A neighboring manor house at *Poturzyn*, c1900

Believed to be the home of the *Wojciechowski* family where *Jerzy* would visit as a child (the house was destroyed by fire during the Second World War)

Samples of letterhead/stationery in use at the *Radostów* and nearby *Terebiniec* manor houses Poland C1900s

The manor house at *'Radostów'* the *Dobiecki* Family home (the main house later destroyed in 1915)

Jerzy's mother, *Konstancja Dobiecka* (left) and great aunt, *Maryja Wiercieńska* (right) Poland, 1910

Konstancja Dobiecka with three of her children, *Janina, Jerzy* (behind) and brother, *Kazimierz* **Poturzyn** 1905

(*Jerzy* (rear right of picture) standing behind his mother and next to other members of the *Dobiecki* family, **Radostów** 1911

Jerzy's youngest brother, *Stanisław Dobiecki*, Poland c1914

Jerzy's sister, *Janina Dobiecka* Poland c1922

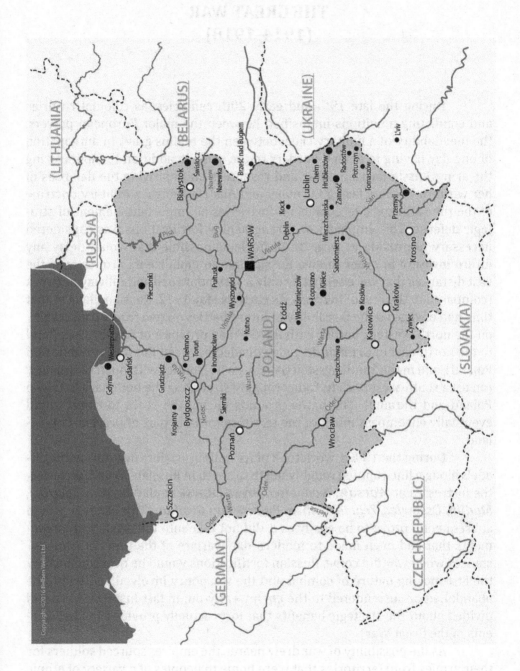

Present-day map of Poland © 2016 Belben Wells UK Ltd

CHAPTER 2
THE GREAT WAR
(1914-1918)

During the late 19th and early 20th centuries, as colonial rivalries and conflicting ambitions intensified between the major European powers, the inevitability of a military clash between the realms grew. In anticipation of one day having to defend borders to the west, in addition to modernizing the army, Russia focused effort and resources on improving the defenses of her western borders facing Germany and Austria-Hungary. Military doctrine of the time still considered ancient fortresses an important element of strategic defense. This emphasis on strengthening fortifications was considered necessary to provide as large an obstacle as possible that would delay any future invasion in order to give Russia time to mobilize its armies over the vast distances that were served by only a very poor road and railway network (compared to the rest of Europe). As early as May 1912, Russian plans at that time had envisaged the possibility of future battles on two fronts if attacked – on the north-western border with the German province of East Prussia (land to the north-east of *Grudziądz*, today divided between Russia, Lithuania and Poland), and in the South-West in Galicia, on its frontier with Austria-Hungary (an area south-west of *L'viv*, today roughly straddling the boundary between Poland and Ukraine). The battle grounds during the years to come would eventually encompass much of the territory forming part of present-day Poland.

During the 1800s, work took place to improve fortifications at the citadels along a line running roughly north to south in Russian Poland, including the fortresses at *Warsaw, Ivanogrod, Brest-Litovsk* (today *Brest* in Belarus), *Modlin, Ossowiec, Zegrze, Łomża, Pułtusk* and *Grodno*. (This strategy would subsequently prove to be costly as it did not take into full account improvements that had been made to modern-day warfare of the time; in some instances when war did come, Russian fortifications would be overwhelmed by the fast-moving nature of combat and the weaponry involved and had to be abandoned or surrendered to the enemy early-on; in fact historians are still divided about the strategic benefits that forts actually provided the belligerents of the Great War).

As the possibility of war drew nearer, the empires sourced soldiers for their armies from territories that were home to peoples of a variety of ethnic and national backgrounds, each with their own mother tongue. In the Austro-Hungarian army, there is an example of orders that would eventually need to be translated to up to fifteen different languages. Approximately 1.9 million Poles would be sent to the fighting in either the Austro-Hungarian, German,

French or Russian armies, in a war that was to have little to do with Poland's Cause but one that many Poles hoped would eventually bring about a re-birth of an autonomous Polish state.

Although there had been no internationally recognized Polish army officially constituted on Polish soil at the time of the outbreak of the Great War, as recently as 1906 throughout Russian Poland there had been limited organized guerilla activity mounted by groups of Poles against the Tsarist regime. A small force of approximately 750 men would eventually metamorphose into what became known as the *Union for Active Struggle* (*Związek Walki Czynnej*), a secret military organization formed by *Kazimierz Sosnkowski* (1885-1969) *Marian Kukiel* (1885-1972) and *Władisław Sikorski* (1881-1943). This formation later became one of the first units of a polish army to be established in an independent Poland at the end of the Great War. (Subsequently, during the Second World War, all three men would continue to play key roles in the creation and leadership of the Polish Army in exile in Great Britain).

In 1914, in Austria-Hungary-controlled Poland, about 12,000 men led by *Józef Pilsudski* (1867-1935) were organized into Polish Legions, formed from para-military sporting associations under the command of Austrian officers of Polish origin and permitted to wear Polish uniforms.

France would give authority for Polish legions to be created on French soil (also later known as the '*Blue Army*' on account of the blue, French uniforms issued to Polish soldiers). A unit of Polish soldiers (*Polska Siła Zbrojna*) known as the *Polnische Wehmacht*, was also later established under Germany's command, led by *Gen. Stanisław Szeptycki* (1867-1950).

Although Russia would later deploy some 82 infantry divisions to the battles of the Great War and had a further sixteen defending the Baltic and Black Sea coastlines, by the end of 1914 and having sustained such high numbers of deaths in the fighting, the Russian authorities announced the formation of two Polish cavalry squadrons, together with Polish legions of approximately 1,000 Poles as part of its own imperial army; these units were allocated to the Russian 59th Defense Brigade, commanded by *Gen. Piotr Szymanowski*. Amongst these formations, the *Puławy Legion*, and the *Lublin Legion* were both made-up of Polish volunteers living in Russian Poland.

The spark that ignited the Great War in Europe would come in June 1914, in Bosnia Herzegovina – a country comprising a mixture of races and formerly a province of the Ottoman empire. Bosnia had become a protectorate of Austria-Hungary in 1908 as the Turkish empire relinquished its hold over the Balkan region of Europe. Having also released itself from its shackles to the Turks, the neighboring independent and predominantly Slav state of Serbia – that shared ethnic and linguistic ties with Bosnia, now sought to liberate all Serbs in the region, and began to be perceived as a threat to Austrian interests.

Whilst on a visit to the Bosnian administrative capital of *Sarajevo*, the heir to the Austrian throne – Archduke *Franz Ferdinand* (1863-1914) who was in the area attending military maneuvers in his capacity as the Inspector General of Austria-Hungary's army, was assassinated by a gunman who had affiliations to an extremist Serbian nationalist group. Although this slaying was but one in a long list of assassinations of heads of state and public dignitaries in Europe since the mid 1880's, on this occasion, given the interconnecting nature and volatility of the different aspects of European politics of that epoch, the shooting precipitated a series of events that would engulf the empires of Europe in war that quickly spread to the rest of the world (see Appendix One for more detail).

Within weeks of the attack in Bosnia, on 28 July 1914, Austria-Hungary declared war on Serbia – in part as a form of retaliation and started a bombardment the following day of the Serbian capital *Belgrade*. The complex system of alliances between states that had been agreed in previous years, led Russia to place its army on a war footing in order to come to the aid of its Slav Serbian comrades, and Germany prepared for a show of strength in support of her ally Austria-Hungary.

And so, began the mobilization and deployment of the Russian army to its own two fronts in 1914, (it took about a month to transfer some troops to the combat zone from their bases in Siberia in the east) and by August the garrison of the Russian 9th Army assembled in **Warsaw**. It was not long before the Russian 1st, 2nd, 3rd, 4th, 8th and 9th Armies were engaging both German and Austro-Hungarian armies over a combat zone stretching roughly 1,000 miles north to south, between *Reval* (today *Tallinn* in Estonia) on the Baltic coast, south as far as **Przemyśl** (south-east Poland) and *Czernowitz* (Romania). Much of the fighting in this part of eastern Europe (referred-to as the 'Eastern Front' of the Great War) would later shift, to-and-fro across modern-day Poland and along the present borders between Poland, Lithuania, Russia, Belarus and the Ukraine. Although trench warfare would characterize the fighting the length of the Western Front, the engagements and offensives along the Eastern Front became much more mobile in nature. The distances covered in the east by advances and retreats were measured in miles rather than in yards.

The broad picture of the main offensives over the forthcoming 36 months on this Eastern Front opened with Austria-Hungary, Russia and Germany transporting and marching their armies across the Polish salient to initially engage one another in the north – in East Prussia and south, in the region of *Galicia*.

Map showing Poland at the outset of the Great War in 1914 and the region of Europe that would become the 'Eastern Front' of the war. (Map © Simon & Schuster UK Ltd)

The Russian 1st and 2nd Armies attacked German lines in East Prussia on 17 August and despite initial success, following a German counter attack in the vicinity of the Mazurian lakes, the Russians were heavily defeated at *Tannenberg* (today near *Olsztyn* in Poland – to the south-east of the Baltic Sea port of **Gdansk**).

By contrast, making gains in the south west, (except for the fortress town of **Przemyśl** which was held by the garrison of Austro-Hungarian troops) the Russian army swept aside the remaining Austro-Hungarian armies back as far as the *Carpathian Mountains* (roughly to the south-east of *L'viv*) before directing effort to reinforce the Russian hold over **Warsaw.**

On 9 October 1914, the German army crossed the River **Vistula** towards **Warsaw** and then had to retreat from the heavily defended city in the face of a Russian counter-offensive. This Russian assault would eventually be halted by a strengthened German army at the battle of **Łódź**, both sides continuing to incur very heavy casualties.

Early in 1915, a German advance – backed by Austro-Hungarian troops, sought to push back Russian positions in the *Carpathian Mountains*. The offensive was initially stalled by the Russians but again, at a high cost of casualties. The fortress town of **Przemyśl** had been besieged by Russian troops since November the previous year, and by March 1915 the Austro-Hungarian troops that had been defending it, capitulated.

In May 1915 *Jerzy* and his brother *Kazimierz* were recruited into the Russian army, at the ages of twenty and nineteen respectively. Beyond a passing mention of the fact as part of his antecedents, it is unfortunately unclear from *Jerzy's* military record which specific regiment he was enlisted in or what role he played whilst in the Russian Imperial Army. He unfortunately never spoke of this period of his military career to the rest of his family. His military records today merely state that he had been deployed to 'the Front' in the Russian Imperial Army, between 1915 and 1917.

A spring offensive, began by German and Austro-Hungarian forces in May, enabled the recapture from Russian control of **Przemyśl** and *Lemburg* (**L'viv**) (albeit both in ruins). By June, the front had moved eastwards by some 100 miles, although **Warsaw** was still firmly under the control of Russian troops. A pincer movement aimed at encircling the city by the central powers during the subsequent **Gorlice-Tarnow** assault in the following months, resulted in a victorious German army entering **Warsaw** on 4 August 1915. Before long, **Warsaw** would become the seat of government for the German occupation of Poland as her armies pushed the Russian army eastwards beyond **Białystok,** *Kowno* and *Brest-Litovsk*. In the void that was left behind the retreating army, during 1916 *Wilhelm II* of Germany (1859-1941) and *Franz Josef I* of Austria (1830-1916) declared the establishment of the Kingdom of Poland – effectively a German zone of occupation.

So as to assist plans for a joint summer offensive on the Western Front by Britain and France, Russia planned to assault German forces in the East and thereby weaken its overall position. In June 1916, led by *Gen. Alexei Brusilow* (1853-1926), Russian troops launched a successful two-pronged attack against the Austrian army in *Galicia* and further north across the river *Bug*. This offensive brought the Austro-Hungarian army close to total collapse. By the end of the year, the German army was nonetheless able to regain most of the ground that had been won by the Russian troops earlier in the summer. This defeat would have profound consequences on Russian morale and the dejection and desperation was mirrored back in Russia where, as near widespread famine took hold, society was beginning to fall apart.

In February and March 1917, strikes and demonstrations in *Petrograd* (today *St Petersburg*) in open opposition to the Tsarist regime, questioned the need for Russia's continued involvement in the fighting of the war. Following the abdication of the increasingly isolated Tsar in March, the Bolshevik movement gradually gained authority over the Russian military machine and by November 1917, sought its complete demobilization. Consequently, as the disaffected army began to fragment, the various Polish legions and other formations attached to the Russian army began to disband and to reorganize. Remnants of some of the Polish detachments that had been re-grouped in Russia during the latter part of the Great War, were also able to find their way back to Poland without becoming directly embroiled in the Russian civil war. In one particular case, the re-formed 5th Polish Rifle Division fighting in Siberia, consisting of about 10,000 Poles under the command of Col. *Kazimierz Rumsza* (1886-1970), found itself surrounded by units of the Red Army. Refusing to surrender and in order to avoid capture, the colonel led his men on a march across Russia, eventually returning to Poland by ship in June 1920. Although neither man knew it at the time, the paths of both *Kazimierz Rumsza* and *Jerzy Dobiecki* would cross thirty or so years later, in a suburb of London and in circumstances that would bring them together as landlord and tenant as well as close friends.

Russia progressively withdrew from the Great War and slowly descended into a civil war of its own. Despite significant German gains on the Eastern Front and as the appetite for yet another winter of war at the end of 1917 began to wane, Germany itself fell victim to strikes and to civil unrest, to mutinies, to desertions from the army and a break-down of law and order at home. In July 1918 the German army was additionally pushed back from the Western Front, having failed in a gamble to end the war in that part of Europe by a prolonged bombardment of allied positions. Disorder broke-out in Berlin and German commanders in *Warsaw*, finding themselves with no orders to act upon, laid-down their arms. The Austrian zone of occupation disintegrated fairly rapidly thereafter, as the numerous ethnic elements of her army simply stopped fighting following successful offensives along the Austrian fronts by French, Italian and Serbian troops.

The three former great powers that had once occupied and controlled Poland, had finally collapsed and the armistice that brought an end to the fighting of the Great War was declared on 11 November 1918. At the Peace Conference at *Versailles* the following year, a fresh map of Poland's borders and frontiers would be fashioned from the mosaic of peoples from many different ethnic groups. As early as 1917 a collection of Poles that had set itself up in France as Poland's 'National Committee' – effectively claiming to be Poland's future government in exile and led by *Roman Dmowski*, received recognition by France, Britain, Italy and America.

Among the eventual measures to feature in the Peace Accord of 1919, were the restoration of an independent Poland and the granting of access by Poland to the Baltic Sea (see Appendix Two, map section at the rear of this book). Despite the cessation of hostilities of the war however, it was not long before the country would once again become entangled in further confrontations with her newly emerging neighboring states.

Kazimierz Dobiecki (Jerzy's brother) wearing the uniform of a junior officer with the Russian Imperial Army, 15 March 1915

CHAPTER 3
RETURN FROM THE FRONT
(1918-1920)

It is known that both *Jerzy* and his brother *Kazimierz* returned to **Radostów,** their family home, from the fighting on the Eastern Front of the Great War sometime during 1918. The de facto government of Poland had reorganized and relocated to France (the 'Polish National Committee') and a temporary, but functioning three-man 'Regency Council', had meanwhile also been established in Warsaw. Having declared Poland an independent Republic, the Council handed full powers of Head of State to Marshal *Józef Piłsudski*, nominating *Jedrzej Moraczewski* (1870-1944) as prime minister.

In 1919, fighting between Polish and Russian troops broke-out in what is known as the Russo-Polish War. The Polish army fought to stop the Russian forces advancing through Poland in its attempt to reclaim Polish territory awarded to Poland by the armistice. Russia was not only seeking to reclaim land that it believed was its own territory but also believed it could now launch a wider crusade to export communism further into western Europe.

This clash between Russia and Poland set the stage for the next scene in *Jerzy's* military career. Unlike his brother, *Kazimierz*, who decided to leave the army and to settle down following the Great War to manage his own estate of *Terebiniec* (situated a few kilometers from **Poturzyn**), Jerzy sought to continue his life in the Polish army and to forge a career as a soldier.

At this point Poland was in chaos after being ravaged by several years of war. Although figures vary, of the estimated one million Poles killed during the Great War, somewhere in the region of 400,000 Poles had lost their lives fighting for one or other of the imperial armies.[1] Just under a million Polish soldiers had been wounded. Polish industry had been paralyzed, unemployment was rife, communications were almost non-existent and nearly half of all the bridges in Poland had been destroyed; poverty and malnutrition among the civilian population was to be found everywhere (in 1919 there was evidence that one third of the Polish population was on the point of starvation)[2] a factor that was made worse by the arrival of the epidemic of Spanish flu. Towns, cities and rural communities had been decimated with eleven million acres of agricultural land devastated. Forced requisitions of goods, conscriptions of men and, in the case of Poland's eastern provinces, forced relocation of entire communities, had drained much of the country's physical and human resources.[3] There were four legal systems in place across the country and six different currencies in operation – not to mention three different administrative and financial systems.[4] A number of different political groups were emerging with considerably different views about how Poland should now be governed. The picture of the country's future constitution was still unclear.

On returning to what was left of his home, *Jerzy* found that during the Russian army's retreat from advancing German forces across south-east Poland in the latter part of the summer of 1915 – a short time after he had left to go to war, a 'scorched earth' policy – whereby towns and villages were destroyed in the wake of the Russian retreat, had left the main building of the manor house at **Radostów** reduced to rubble. It had been burned to the ground. As a consequence, the family had since moved into and were living in the adjacent annex.

On 1 November 1918, Jerzy enlisted as a senior light cavalryman with the volunteer squadron of the recently formed, *1st Polish Light Cavalry Regiment – the '1. Pułk Szwoleżerów'*. This preceded, by a matter of weeks, Germany's surrender to the Allies on 11th November 1918 (since celebrated as Independence Day in Poland). Although the new Polish Army was officially created around this time, the first independent Polish military units had previously been organized from October 1918 – a month before the November armistice. One of the first commanders of the army – Chief of the General Staff Maj. Gen. *Tadeusz Rozwadowski* (1866-1928), who now reported to the Polish Minister of Military Affairs in Warsaw (Gen. *Rydz-Śmigły* (1886-1941). Both had been generals in the former Austro-Hungarian army.

Among the numerous challenges facing Polish army's High Command at this time, was the task of integrating thousands of soldiers from different military backgrounds into the newly-formed Polish national army. Soldiers were carrying arms and ammunition manufactured in as many as five different countries. In some instances, soldiers found themselves under the command of officers whom they had previously been fighting in opposing armies. Suspicions were rife. The new Polish army was drawn from volunteers previously enlisted in the Austro-Hungarian legions, from the Polish Corps serving in Russia, from the many volunteers of the clandestine *'Polish Military Organization'* (*'Polska Organizacja Wojskowa'*), from amongst men of the corps serving in Germany, from returning troops who had served with the Polish Army in France and from the volunteer militiamen of the Lithuanian and Belarussian Self-Defense Force.[5]

Three months after *Jerzy* joined the *1st Polish Light Cavalry Regiment*, the Army Law of 26 February 1919 restructured the army into five military Districts, those of '**Kraków**', '**Łódź**', '**Lublin**', '**Kielce**' and '**Warsaw**'. Poland's cavalry was reorganized into fourteen new cavalry regiments and subsequently into six cavalry brigades. Conscription into the army was reintroduced on 7 March 1919. As important as standardization was, much of the army's restructuring was necessary in order to meet the need to immediately deploy to the six wars that had to be fought in order to determine the new Polish Republic's borders. From November 1918, Poland fought battles with forces of the West Ukrainian Republic and from December, engaged with German troops for control of the area around **Poznań** and *Silesia*. In January 1919, following the takeover of *Cieszyn*, Poland was drawn into a war with Czechoslovakia. As early as February 1919, following the German withdrawal from Poland, the first skirmishes occurred in the Russo-Polish war over her eastern borders. In July 1919, Poland confronted Lithuanian forces over the disputed possession of the city of *Wilno* (***Vilnius***). Although the Great War had been concluded by the Treaty of Versailles (ratified by Poland in 1919), battles actually continued in Poland over the final settlement of its borders until the signing of the Polish-Soviet Peace Treaty, as late as March 1921.

Between November 1919 and March 1920, *Jerzy* attended Cavalry Class No. 23 at the Infantry Officer School in ***Warsaw***. For the following two months, between March and 1 May 1920, he took part in further training at the Cavalry Officer School in ***Przemyśl*** in south-east Poland. As an Officer Cadet, on 1 May 1920, he was transferred to the 18th Polish Pomeranian Lancers Regiment – formed only the year previously and was stationed in ***Grudziądz*** where he became a Platoon Leader (see Appendix 4(A)).

Regimental badge of the 1st Polish Light Cavalry Regiment – '1. Pułk Szwoleżerów' – The Józef Piłsudski Regiment (Jerzy's regiment between 1 November 1918 and November 1919)

Jerzy Dobiecki, Officer Cadet, Cavalry Officer School, *Przemyśl*, Poland 1920

Ian von Heintze

CHAPTER 4
FORMATION OF THE 18TH POLISH POMERANIAN LANCERS REGIMENT[1]
(1919-1920)

The 18th Polish Pomeranian Lancers Regiment was created as a regiment of the Polish army on 24 July 1919. A military order, signed by Gen. *Dowbor-Muśnicki* (1867-1937), the officer commanding forces in Poland's province of *Wielkopolska* ('Greater Poland'), set-out the procedures for the recruitment and assembly of a force of men from in and around the city of **Poznań** – located in the region of Pomerania in north-west Poland. At the time, this area and that of neighboring Polish *Masuria* were still recovering from German-Prussian occupation. With the consequent suspicion and general mistrust felt by Polish communities in these regions, the appeal for men to join a new, independent Polish regiment initially circulated amongst townsfolk in an atmosphere of some secrecy. To the Poles living in this part of Poland however, this call to arms heralded the confirmation of a return of *Pomerania* to Polish control, as this part of Poland had been subjected to direct control by Prussia since 1871. Large numbers of volunteers – many of whom had made the dangerous journey from beyond the Polish-German demarcation line, began to muster at the new regiment's rallying points. Impoverished as a result of the war, Poland's funding of this recruitment-drive was initially heavily reliant upon donations to the cause made by local townsfolk. These small communities very much took to-heart, the formation of a Polish Ułan ('lancers' or 'troopers')[2] regiment in their midst.

During the first month of the regiment's formation, it was known as the '*4-ty Pułk Ułanów Wielkopolskich*' – the *4th Greater Poland Lancers Regiment* and then titled '*Nadwiślański Pułk Ułanów*' – *the Vistula Ułan Regiment.* Although the unit was using the title as early as 1 August 1919, it was not until the following year - the 5 March 1920, that the designated name of '*18-ty Pułk Ułanów Pomorskich*' – the *18th Polish Pomeranian Lancers Regiment*, was officially approved. In accordance with uniform regulations of the day, the Ułans of the *18th Pomeranian Lancers* were issued with peaked "*Rogatywki*" – distinctive Polish square-crowned, peaked caps with a sky-blue band wrapped around its circumference. Pennant insignia worn on jacket collars and lance pennons attached to the lances carried by troopers, comprised horizontal white over sky-blue strips separated by a scarlet flash. Shoulder epaulettes bore the number '18' just below the insignia of rank.

Although the regiment was initially raised in **Poznań**, it would eventually be relocated to **Toruń** and thereafter to the city of *Graudenz* – after the city had been returned to Polish control (at which point the city has become known as '**Grudziądz**').

The responsibility for the regiment's formation was given to its first commanding officer, *Lt. Col. August Donimirski*. Among the other officers initially appointed to the regiment were Cavalry *Capt. Stanisław Ossowski, Lt. Kazimierz Prandota- Trzciński* and *2nd Lts. Władysław Buschke* and *Klemens Zieliński*.

In September 1919, *Lt. Colonel Donimirski* was appointed to the post of Inspector General of the Volunteer Army in the Military District of Pomerania. His functions at the head of the regiment were taken over by *Col. Rudolf Alzner*. The day-to-day logistics involved in the actual formation of the regiment were delegated to Cavalry *Capt. Ossowski* who, by October 1919 had formed the 1st Squadron – comprising three platoons; each platoon was made up of four sections and each section contained six troopers with six horses.

During Inspections carried out in October 1919, the regiment was to be commended for its turn-out during training by *Gen. Józef Haller* (1873-1960) and by Poland's Commander-in-Chief, *Marshal Józef Piłsudski*.

On 16 January 1920, during the campaign to recover the north-western region of Pomerania from German control, the first squadron of the *18th Polish Pomeranian Lancers* – led by *Capt. Ossowski* with 4 officers, 180 troopers equipped with 'Mauser' rifles and sabers (and with 2 light machine guns in support), marched out of **Poznań** to take up a position as the advance-guard to the Pomeranian Infantry Division of *Col. Skrzyński*. The regiment held its own during an early encounter with units of the 'Grenzschutz' (German Border Guard) prior to its return to **Toruń** where a second squadron was formed. Jerzy Dobiecki would join this unit four months later.

Troopers (Ułans) of the Pułk Ułanów Nadwiślańskich, The Vistula Lancers Regiment, Poland c1919
(from the private collection of Sławomir Ziętarski © Sławomir Ziętarski)

1-szy szwadron 4-go Pułku Ułanów Nadwiślańskich w Poznaniu. Officers and men of the 1st squadron of 4th Polish Vistula Lancers Regiment, Poznań c1919
(from the private collection of Sławomir Ziętarski © Sławomir Ziętarski)

Cavalry *Captain Ossowski*, 18th Polish Pomeranian Lancers, c1919
(from the private collection of *Sławomir Ziętarski* © Sławomir Ziętarski)

The 1st squadron, 18th Polish Pomeranian Lancers, entering Toruń in January 1920. March-past along the Szeroka Street. At the head of the column, the commander of the squadron, Cavalry Captain Stanisław Ossowski.
(from the private collection of Sławomir Ziętarski © Sławomir Ziętarski)

Second Lieutenant *Sławomir de Latour*, (mounted) 18th Polish Pomeranian Lancers, at the gate of the fortress in *Grudziądz*, 1919
(from the collection of *Lesław Kukawski*)
(image supplied by kind permission of *Sławomir Ziętarski*)

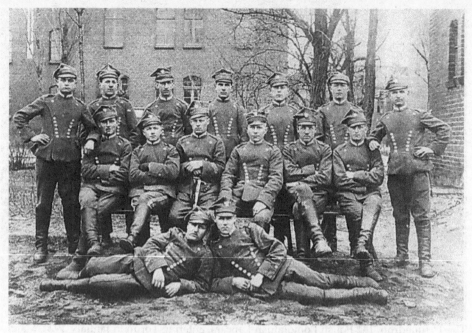

Group of junior officers and lancers of the 18th Polish Pomeranian Lancers Poland, 1920.
(image supplied by kind permission of Sławomir Ziętarski © Sławomir Ziętarski)

CHAPTER 5
THE POLISH-RUSSIAN FRONT – BELARUS & LATVIA
(1920)

Following the Russian westward offensive in what had by then become the Russo-Polish War, Polish forces had confronted the Russian army since February of 1919. *Jerzy* was officially transferred to the 18th Polish Pomeranian Lancers on 1 May 1920, and that same month the 1st Squadron of the regiment – commanded by Cavalry Capt. *Stanisław Ossowski,* was brought up to strength. After completing maneuvers, the regiment was assigned to reinforce other units of the Polish army that had been engaging Russian troops in the north-east of the country at one of Poland's two 'Fronts' in this war (see Appendix 2-Map 5). Despite the Peace Treaty at the conclusion of the Great War a year earlier, Poland's eastern borders were far from being settled. A line in the sand had of course been drawn to reflect where the border might be located between Poland and Russia, later known as the 'Curzon' Line. This demarcation and provisional border between Poland and the Soviet republics to the east, had attempted to take account of the locations of the greatest concentrations of ethnic Poles.

It was against this background that, as a member of one of two squadrons of the 18th Pomeranian Lancers, *Jerzy's* departure to the Front as an officer cadet was announced. A battalion, comprising the first and second squadrons, made up of 2 officers, 8 officer cadets and 162 troopers equipped with small arms, supported by 3 heavy machine guns departed for the Northern Front on 29 May 1920. The battalion was directed to link-up with the 1st Cavalry Brigade of the "*Dźwina* Operational Group" commanded by Gen. *Sosnkowski*. This latter cavalry brigade was operating in the border regions of Latvia, Belarus and Lithuania, in the basin of the river *Dźwina* (today called the River *Daugava*). Fighting was heavy along the entire Front. Units of the 15th Russian Army reportedly vastly outnumbered the Polish troops in the zone and on 14 and 15 May, had begun an offensive against Polish units in the direction of Mołodeczno (**Maladzyechna**, present-day Belarus). A reserve army of Polish units had been established in the vicinity of *Święciany*, under Gen. *Sosnkowski's* command, with the objective of striking the northern flank of the attacking Army.

Jerzy's regiment, with its horses and ancilliary equipment, together with the Polish 7th and 11th Lancer regiments, the 1st Light Cavalry Regiment and the 1st Mounted Artillery Battalion, were transported into the theatre of operations by train – eventually alighting at the station at **Turmanty** (*Turmantas* in modern-day Lithuania, see map at the end of this chapter).

A week passed before the regiment set-off towards the vicinity of **Miory** (in present-day Latvia) on 5 June 1920. Deployed on the right flank of the brigade's advance, the following day the battalion started to patrol a line between *Genopol – Sawczenki – Drygucze* and in this way, closed the narrow pass between the **Dźwina** River and the marshes of a nearby Lake, the *Jełań*. Simultaneously, the Polish 11th Lancers Regiment was deployed on the brigade's left flank.

On 6 June, the battalion passed through the villages of *Robowo, Bukowo* and *Pieczonki* and received word of enemy activity at nearby **Miory** manor farm, near *Stanielowo*. In a pincer movement, the 1st squadron of the 18th Pomeranian Lancers (having dismounted at the Miory manor farm) engaged the opposing lines, pushing these units south towards the small town of Miory where the bulk of the Russian battalion was positioned. The 2nd squadron of the 18th Pomeranian Lancers, commanded by Officer Cadet *Roszczynialski* deployed from the south-west, outflanking the Russian battalion. Although the maneuver forced the retreat of the Russian units and enabled the seizure of Miory, the action resulted in the death of trooper *Stefan Sarnowski*.

A further engagement occurred between units of the regiment and sections of two battalions of the 490th Russian Infantry Regiment and, following a short encounter at the *Czeress* manor farm, the enemy was again driven back, enabling the 18th Pomeranian Lancers squadrons that had remained intact to reach the small town of *Czeress* itself.

The following day, on 7th June and whilst redeploying at *Wielka Kowalewszczyzna*, my grandfather's battalion received orders to press forward in the direction of the northern marshes of *Lake Jełań*, in order to engage the rear of the eastward-retreating Russian units. Whilst negotiating difficult terrain and completely unexpectedly, *Jerzy* and the battalion were drawn into a skirmish with units of opposing army reserves, sustaining a number of casualties. In a surprise attack from all sides and whilst in wooded countryside, many of the squadron's horses were startled by close-quarter gun-fire and bolted towards the enemy positions, unsaddling their riders.

Whilst the 2nd squadron retreated on horseback, the now largely dismounted 1st squadron, after engaging the remaining Russian units for several hours, was itself forced to retreat through the woods before it was able to rejoin the remainder of the battalion.

The battalion returned to the town of *Czeress* to re-group for an overnight stay and most of the loose horses of the 1st squadron were eventually rounded-up. That day, the battalion sustained 7 soldiers wounded with 17 horses killed. Two enemy machine guns were captured. Together with the commander of the 1st squadron, Lt. *Trzciński*, Officer Cadet *Dobiecki*, Corpl. *Dabiński* and Trooper *Gertig* each received commendations for bravery.

On 9 June, Lt. *Trzciński* set-off with the 2nd squadron to reinforce the 11th Lancers Regiment. On arrival at the village of *Denisowo* and having come under enemy fire, it joined the 7th and 11th Lancer regiments taking-up positions near the village of *Wianuża*. During the night of 10 June, having held its position for 24 hours, once reinforcements had arrived to strengthen units entrenched in the marshes near the *Jelnia* Lake and the **Dźwina** River, the squadron fell back to the safety of the lines of ensconced Polish infantry.

When units of the 15th Russian Army had retreated beyond the *Berezyna* and *Auta* rivers, the Polish 1st Mounted Brigade was dispatched further south, leaving behind the battalion of the 18th Pomeranian Lancers at the **Dźwina** River. The battalion was now assigned for the rest of that month to the 15th Brigade of the 8th Polish Infantry Division. This unit was patrolling the banks of the River **Dźwina** between the village of *Usmena* near *Dryssa* (today *Verkhnyadzvinsk* in Belarus) and the village of *Drygucze*, where units of the Polish army were dug-in. Coincidentally, *Usmena* was being used at this time to garrison units of the Latvian army.

On 27 June, Officer Cadet *Juliusz Chmielowski*, accompanied by three troopers were sent across the river to reconnoiter. Whilst approaching the outskirts of the village of *Usmena,* they came upon a large number of Russian infantrymen who were evidently planning an ambush and had been crouching in fields of crops on the perimeter of the village. Realizing that a surprise attack on the village was imminent and that his own patrol was seriously outnumbered, *Chmielowski* abruptly started to bellow orders and commands at the top of his voice in an attempt to make it appear that he was accompanied by a huge attacking force of Polish cavalry. Officer Cadet *Chmielowski* repeatedly barked commands at the Russians to surrender. The ruse was successful. Suddenly infantrymen began to break cover from all corners of the field and could be seen running into the distance. The Russian soldiers nearest the Polish horses surrendered, dropping their weapons as they gave themselves up. Three prisoners were taken back across the river to the Polish lines for interrogation.

During the stopover at the **Dźwina** River, the battalion was struck by an outbreak of dysentery and, on 25 June, Cavalry Cap. *Ossowski* had to be evacuated to a field hospital. The command of the regiment was taken over by Lt. *Trzciński* and Officer Cadet *Emich* took charge of the 1st squadron. The 2nd squadron was to be commanded by Lt. *Tadeusz Mincer.*

At a certain point during the night of 3/4 July, the Russian army launched an offensive that broke through several places along the Polish front, driving the Polish 15th Brigade into retreat from its original position between the **Dźwina** River and Lake **Jelnia**. Fearful of being cut off from the south, troops of the Polish 8th Division – under pressure from significantly larger enemy forces, also retreated from positions between *Usmeny – Drygucze – Genopol*. They held a defensive position near a number of lakes in the *Przebrodzie* area and a short distance from the confluence of the Rivers **Dźwina** and *Wiata*.

The 1st battalion of the 18th Pomeranian Lancers was now allocated a ten-kilometer stretch of the *Wiata* River to patrol, between the **Dźwi-**

na river in the north as far as the town of *Szelągi*, where the Polish infantry was in place. Following the retreat of the 8th Infantry Division on the 4 July, the mounted battalion held its position despite coming under sustained and heavy fire. At around this time the town of **Maladzyechna** was captured by units commanded by Gen. *Stanisław Szeptycki*. During the early hours of 5 July, near the village of *Soromszczyzna*, Lt. *Tadeusz Mincer* made his indelible mark on the 18th Pomeranian Lancers regiment's short history. Having been shot three times, he continued to command the second squadron. Only when he lost consciousness after being shot for a fourth time was he removed from the battle for medical treatment.

In order to improve the operational capability of the battalion, its commander – Lt. *Trzciński*, ordered that all rider-less horses should be returned to the rear of the Polish lines. The responsibility for herding the horses back to safety was given to *Jerzy*. Shortly following his departure, accompanied by the horses and several riders, the remainder of the battalion was surrounded near the town of *Druja* and outflanked by units of cavalry belonging to the Russian III Cavalry Corps, commanded by *Hayk Bzhishkyan* (1887-1937). Having their backs to the River **Dźwina** and now being cut off to the south as well as to the west and despite several unsuccessful attempts to break through the Russian defenses, the decision was taken to swim across the river and thereby to cross into Latvia. The aim was to reach **Dyneburg** (now '*Daugavpils*' in Latvia) and to join-up with other Polish troops stationed to the south of the city. As the rest of the battalion crossed the river, one of the platoons with three machine guns and under the command of Officer Cadet Emich was left in place in **Druja** to provide covering fire.

Trooper *Bernard Strzelecki,* who was the first to try and swim across the river, together with three Latvian cavalrymen from the liaison patrol assigned to the battalion, drowned after losing their fight with the overwhelming current. Several horses were also swept away and perished.

It wasn't long before *Jerzy* and his men, together with the loose horses, would also become cut-off from the battalion as they came accross Russian cavalry patrols near Lake **Snudy**. *Jerzy* was forced to make a similar decision and together with the loose horses forded the **Dźwina** river, taking his unit to **Dyneburg** to be re-united with the battalion the following day.

At the time that the battalion and hundreds of other Poles sought refuge in Latvia, they were welcomed with open arms. Indeed, so many Polish soldiers were fleeing from the advancing Russian army that an entire infantry battalion was assembled there, initially under the command of Infantry Lt. *Zatryba* and then Infantry Lt. *Strugała*.

The Commander of the Polish military mission in Latvia stationed in **Riga** – Capt. *Myszkowski*, immediately went about arrangements for the repatriation to Poland of the Polish troops, including *Jerzy's* stranded unit. The efforts were nonetheless met with resistance from the Latvian authorities, intent upon disarming the battalion and seeking to impound the regiment's horses and equipment. Orders from **Riga** arrived several weeks later and on 22 July the battalion was transferred to *Libawa* (**Liepāja**) on the coast of Latvia, where it arrived on 26 July.

The Russian Army in the meantime, had continued its advance and had by then made gains as far as the River **Bug**.

On 30 July, the Polish ship '*Pomorzanin*' (the 'Pomeranian') arrived at **Liepāja** from **Gdańsk** on the Polish coast. Restricted by its size, it was only able to accommodate sixty infantrymen and not the riders and their horses of the mounted regiments. Officer Cadet *Chądzyński* of the 18th Pomeranian Lancers nevertheless dismounted and boarded the ship in order to travel with the vessel to Poland, to do what he could on arrival there to ensure the eventual safe return of his stranded unit.

On 11 August 1920 at noon, with no further news having been received from Poland or from **Riga**, the Polish battalion commander at **Liepāja** was informed that Latvia had signed a treaty with Russia and that the battalion was to be disarmed forthwith. Being keen to avoid such an eventuality at all costs, Lt. *Trzciński* arranged to leave Liepāja, immediately without informing the Latvian authorities and with the intention of breaking through to the free city of *Kłajpeda* (**Klaipėda** in modern day Lithuania).

During the early hours of 12 August, the Polish unit of the 18th Pomeranian Lancers and horses set off under the cover of darkness to reach *Pałąga* (**Palanga**) a few hours later. There, they learned that too many hostile Lithuanian troops were garrisoned in the area and further progress undetected would not be possible. The units therefore took shelter and hid in the woods of *Zelwa* manor farm near **Palanga**, receiving food and horse-feed from local Latvians. Eventually and having run out of options, the battalion was forced to retrace its steps back to **Liepāja** where, very reluctantly, the unit did hand-over its weapons to the Latvian authorities.

By now the Polish cavalrymen were quite disheveled and many were dressed in torn and tattered civilian clothes, handed-out to them from supplies kept by the American Red Cross station in Latvia. Upon the arrival of the Polish ship '*Saratov*' a few days later, Lt. *Trzciński* and as many members of the regiment as could be accommodated, boarded the ship and set sail for the port of **Gdańsk**. The remainder of the battalion that was left behind, under *Jerzy's* command, remained in nearby *Zelwa* where preparations were made in anticipation of an imminent return to Poland.

At dusk on 15 August, the remainder of the battalion was able to embark the '*Pomorzanin*' which departed for Poland in a raging gale. The weather was so bad at sea that the ship's captain – Lt. *Bramiński*, decided to put into the port of **Kłajpeda** to take shelter from the threatening swell.

On 18 August, both the '*Saratov*' and the '*Pomorzanin*' sailed to the Polish haven of **Gdańsk** but were unable to dock there on arrival due to a strike by port-workers. This forced the ships to sail on to and disembark at **Gdynia**, a little further along the Polish coast.

Following three days of rest and recuperation, the battalion marched to *Kartuzy* where the unit boarded a train to the garrison headquarters at **Toruń**. The battalion finally arrived there on 22 August.

During the first days of August 1920, while *Jerzy's* battalion had been on operations in the north, the regiment's 2nd battalion, commanded by Maj. *Iwanow*, had also been deployed to the front and was attached to the volunteer division of Col. *Adam Koc*. A number of intensively fought rear-guard actions, advances and skirmishes took their toll on the battalion that forced its return to barracks in mid-September for reorganization. Among others, remarkable bravery had been demonstrated by Lt. *Bolesław Rzępołuch*, the commander of the squadron, who was killed in action in a battle at the village of *Pruszki* on 15 August 1920. Special recognition was also given to 2nd Lts. *Mikołaj Iznoskoff, Edward Łęcki* and Officer Cadet *Witold Skarżyński*.

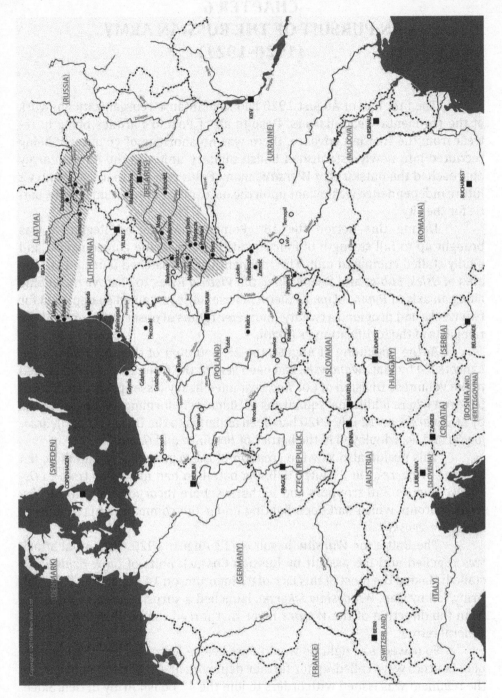

The 18th Polish Pomeranian Lancers Regiment areas of operation,
Russo-Polish War 1920-1921
(Against background of present-day States of Europe)
© 2016 Belben Wells UK Ltd

CHAPTER 6
IN PURSUIT OF THE RUSSIAN ARMY
(1920-1921)

The first half of August 1920 had seen intense reorganizational work at the regimental headquarters. Despite all of Poland's armies being in retreat from the Russian advance, there was no shortage of volunteers being recruited into newly-established Polish military units. As the Russian army approached the outskirts of **Warsaw**, many Poles realized that the country's future independence was reliant upon the outcome of the now inevitable, battle for the city.

During this period the 18th Pomeranian Lancers Regiment was brought up to full strength of four squadrons, a machine gun squadron and a fully staffed command unit. The regiment had dispatched four units to the area of *Osiek, Lubicz* and *Szylno* along the **Vistula** River, to observe the enemy along an axis of *Rypin – Lipno – Sierpc*. These units remained so deployed for two weeks and provided a twenty-kilometer radius of observation around the ramparts of the fortification in **Toruń**.

At the beginning of August, the 2nd battalion of the 18th Pomeranian Lancers led by Maj. *Iwanowski*, had been sent to the front and whilst attached to the Volunteer Division of Col. *Koc*, sustained heavy losses prior to its return to Toruń where additional squadrons of Ułans were forming. One of these, led by Lt. *Bojarski*, on 12 July 1920 had been assigned to the Group of Gen. *Jędrzejowski* and was deployed in the battles of *Brodnica* and *Golub*.

This period also saw the creation of the regiment's 3rd battalion, led by Capt. *Wicherek*. On 29 July 1920, the battalion had moved by train to *Ostrołęka* and its 250 troopers and 92 horses were incorporated into the *Ostrołęka* Group, which had been fighting under the command of Lt. Col. *Jerzy Ferek-Błeszyński*.

The Battle for **Warsaw** began on 13 August 1920. The initial attack was repelled and the assault by Russian Cossack units of *Gayk Bzhishkyan* stalled. Making the most of this lack of momentum, on 14 August the Polish 5th Army, led by Gen. *Władysław Sikorski*, launched a surprise counter-offensive from the direction of the **Wieprz** River that forced the Russian army into a general retreat.

Four weeks of fighting would pass before Jerzy and the 18th Pomeranian Lancers were called-up for further deployment. On 15 September 1920, the regiment was issued with orders to join the 4th Polish Army of Gen. *Skierski* (1866-1940). Commanded by Col. *Rudolf Alzner*, Jerzy and units of the 18th Pomeranian Lancers were transported by train to *Hajnówka* and *Narewka*. Arriving there four days later on 19 September, the 19 officers, 9 officer cadets, 518 troopers, 495 horses, 6 heavy and 6 light machine guns of the regiment were assigned to the operational group of Gen. *Jung* of the 15th Infantry Division. The regiment's battalions were commanded by Majors *Anatol Jezierski* and *Zagłoba Smoleński*. The 1st squadron was commanded by Lt. *Trzciński*, the 2nd squadron by Lt. **Zieliński**, the 4th squadron by Lt. *Monwid- Olechnowicz* and the machine gun squadron by Cavalry Capt. *Wicherek*. The regiment's 3*rd* squadron, comprising 2 officers, 2 officer cadets, 112 troopers and 115 horses, commanded by Cavalry Capt. *Nestorowicz*, was placed at the disposal of the 16th Polish Infantry Division.

Having disembarked from the carriages on 19 September 1920, units of the 18th Polish Pomeranian Lancers crossed the Białowieża Forest and stopped in Pieniążki where they received the following orders on 22 September 1920:

"...Within the operational area commanded by General Jung, in the region of Prużany, units of the 163rd and 165th Russian Infantry Brigades and 142nd and 151st Russian Brigades are in retreat along the axis: Prużany – Łyskowo – Nowy Dwór.

The units of the Operational Group, commanded by General Jung, are to re-group on the line of Nowy Dwór – Bierniki – Łaszewicze, to the north of Świsłocz. In one day, they are commanded to take Wołkowysk (Vawkavysk).

The 18th Pomeranian Lancers Regiment, together with 2 battalions of the 59th Infantry Regiment and 1 battery of the 15th Field Artillery Regiment from Józefin, are to take Nowy Dwór...."

Acting on this Order, *Jerzy* and the 18th Pomeranian Lancers set off from *Pieniążki* at 4pm on 22 September. Passing *Popielewszczyzna, Heleny, Kłetno* and *Radeck*, the Lancers arrived in *Józefin*, where they found only one company of the 59th Regiment engaging the enemy. The Russian forces had dug-in along the route to **Nowy Dwór**. Laying down rapid, heavy fire, the column advanced with, at its head, a dismounted platoon of the 1st squadron commanded by *Jerzy*, supported closely by the remainder of the 1st and the whole of the 2nd Squadron – also dismounted.

After a three-hour battle, the column forced its way along the route to arrive in *Ludwinowo*. Patrols were sent forward from the 1st squadron to **Nowy Dwór**, located 4-5 kilometers away. On their return, they reported that the village had been garrisoned by two regiments of Russian infantry. As the column once again moved towards **Nowy Dwór**, *Jerzy's* patrol came under very heavy, close-quarter fire. Trooper *Jedliński* suffered serious wounds and one horse was killed.

Despite not being able to receive the support of the two battalions of the 59th Regiment as had been previously planned, instructions were given nonetheless to continue the attack on **Nowy Dwór** and, dismounted, the 2nd squadron and part of the 1st, supported by 4 machine guns commanded by Lt. *Zieliński*, continued to move forward. Whilst one platoon of the 2nd squadron laid down covering fire, the other platoon of the 2nd squadron with two machine guns under the command of Officer Cadet *Roszczynialski*, attacked the village from the south side. Simultaneously, the rest of the 1st squadron – with 2 machine guns, advanced from the north using natural cover, to within about 300-400 paces of the village perimeter. Acting together, both squadrons opened fire in the direction of the entrenched Russian troops. Surprised and overwhelmed by the assault, the Russian soldiers withdrew.

Second Lieutenant *Kłopotowski* used the opportunity to move into the village to complete the attack. Despite being hugely outnumbered, the assault on the village succeeded. Approximately 120 prisoners were taken and several carts containing an assortment of arms and ammunition were seized.

The battle of **Nowy Dwór** brought distinction on the regiment and its actions were subsequently honored on the regimental standard. Commended for their bravery were, 2nd Lt. *Michał Kłopotowski*, Officer Cadets *Hipolit Roszczynialski, Jerzy Dobiecki, Stanisław Bydłowski, Henryk Niezabitowski* and Platoon Leaders *Florentyn Dabiński, Jan Hillar, Leon Cieślicki* and Corpl. *Wincenty Zalewski*.

As the Poles continued to push the Russian army further into retreat, another operation was mounted on **Wołkowysk**. The 18th Pomeranian Lancers were now tasked to press forward with orders to cut off the potential Russian retreat to *Zelwa* in the *Wiśniówka* area.

After marching all night on 23 and 24 September and a further march for most of the following day, the regiment encountered units of the 27th Russian Infantry Division heading for **Wołkowysk**. Commanded by 2nd Lt. *Kłopotowski,* as the Lancers' lead unit entered the village of *Krzesła* (3 km south of *Wiśniówka*), it became obvious that Russian infantry had set-up camp a little further into the village. *Kłopotowski* ordered his mounted unit to advance in a charge that was to catch the troops off-guard, although he soon realized that the opposing numbers were greater than he had expected. Suffering a serious wound to the hand, he called a retreat and withdrew from the village back to the Polish lines.

Once it had been briefed about troop emplacements, the remaining units of the 18th Pomeranian Lancers advanced towards the village. The now dismounted 1st squadron launched an attack, reinforced by the 4th machine gun squadron. Initially, the Russian soldiers started to retreat in the face of the barrage of fire but before long responded with a counter attack. This forced the 18th Pomeranian Lancers to withdraw and to look for a weaker point in the Russian positions to try to break through.

At the same time, operating on the regiment's right flank, the mounted 2nd squadron seized the village of **Klepacze** where a significant number of prisoners were taken. Despite eventually having to withdraw in the face of superior numbers, the surprise and repeated testing of the opposition by the regiment spread sufficient confusion amongst Russian units advancing on **Wołkowysk** to make the mopping-up operation by other Polish units easier to execute.

During the two-day raid, Corp. *Franciszek Szymański* and troopers *Kazimierz Trojanowski* and *Jan Mitag* were killed. Second Lieutenant *Kłopotowski*, 5 officer cadets and 14 troopers were wounded. In total, approximately 250 Russian prisoners were captured. Lieutenants *Trzciński* and *Zieliński* and 2nd Lts *Kłopotowski* and *Buterlewicz* earned recognition for their actions during that raid.

As the 15th Polish Infantry Division continued its advance, pushing the Russian army further eastwards, it wasn't long before the Polish troops reached a line of trenches that had been used during the Great War, between the villages of *Miechowicze* and *Skrobowo* (at the source of the *Serwecz* River). Here, units of Russian infantry had taken cover and had set-up a defensive position taking full advantage of the concealment provided by the trenches.

On 2 October, after numerous efforts failed by the Polish artillery and infantry to dislodge the Russian troops, the Divisional commander, Gen. *Jung*, decided to mount a cavalry charge in an attempt to remove the enemy. As the artillery prepared to lay down a barrage of covering fire, the 1st squadron of the 18th Pomeranian Lancers received the order to attack.

Lieutenant *Trzciński*, having led his squadron out of the forest, deployed *Jerzy* and a column of three platoons towards the entrenched Russian positions. Despite very uneven terrain, riddled with small ditches and undergrowth, the cavalry unit's advance made good progress and gathered momentum as it covered the two kilometers of open ground that had to be crossed to reach the trenches. By the time the advancing cavalry had reached the road between *Horodyszcze* (*Haradzišča*) and *Połoneczka*, the charge had started. Simultaneously, Polish artillery fire began pounding the dugouts. Once in sight of the enemy positions, with sabre drawn, *Jerzy* was at the head of his platoon as the charge increased to a full gallop. Despite being met with a volley of machine-gun fire, the troopers maintained their charge, careering toward the trenches. The sight of so many horsemen charging in their direction together with the artillery shells raining down upon them, succeeded in dislodging the entrenched Russian troops. As more Polish squadrons reached the trenches, the Lancers completed the maneuver by opening fire and securing the now vacated ground.

This cavalry charge cost the lives of troopers *Czajkowski* and *Pietras*. Lieutenants *Buterlewicz* and *Monwid-Olechnowicz*, Officer Cadet *Chmielowski* and 13 troopers were wounded. *Jerzy Dobiecki* had his horse shot from under him, and fifteen other horses were either killed or wounded. During the engagement, the 2nd squadron captured 2 two machine guns.

In a subsequent dispatch from Gen. *Jung*, the 18th Pomeranian Lancers were commended for their actions. His dispatch reads:

"...The 18th Pomeranian Lancers Regiment operated within my Group and was given the challenging task of disrupting the Bolshevik offensive at **Wołkowysk***. The regiment pursued the fleeing Bolshevik units and succeeded in depriving them of the opportunity to re-group behind the trench lines.*

During the first operation, the 18th Lancers Regiment fulfilled its task admirably, defending the right flank of the Group; during the battle at Krzesła, it spread confusion within the 27th Russian Division making the situation easier for the Polish 29th Infantry Brigade to engage the enemy.

During the course of the second operation, with the daring charge at Skrobowo and the pursuit from Iszkołdź, the regiment greatly contributed to the dispersal of the enemy.

On behalf of the service, I would like to acknowledge and to thank all the officers and Ułans of the 18th Regiment of Pomeranian Lancers - especially the Commander of the regiment, Major Jezierski and the wounded officers: Lieutenants M. Olechnowicz and 2nd Lieutenants Buterlewicz and Kłopotowski – and I would like to wish them good luck and success in their continued service for the glory of the Fatherland.
Signed
A. Jung
Lieut. General,
Officer Commanding the Operational Group..."

During a period of continued pressure on the retreating Russian army at all points in the area of the upper **Niemen** River, near *Nowy Świerżeń* the 1st squadron captured three cannons and a significant amount of artillery ordnance.

For a short period, the regiment was deployed under the command of Col. *Ignacy Mielżyński*'s cavalry group with the 215th Lancers Regiment, before being redeployed once again with the 16th Pomeranian Infantry Division.

On 14 and 15 October, the regiment was engaged in battles near *Pereszewo* and *Kamionka*. Having crossed the *Łosza* river and taken the town of *Łosza* itself, on 16 October the regiment reached *Tołkaczewice* and *Szack* which were seized following a charge by the 1st squadron.

Towards the end of October, upon receipt of information that a ceasefire had been agreed, the regiment moved to a demarcation line along the axis of *Korżuny, Pukowo, Kamień,* **Zamość***, Rudnia*. The regiment's Command unit and two of its squadrons were stationed at *Onufryjewicze* and the other two squadrons were moved to *Starzyca*.

Members of the 18th Polish Pomeranian Lancers Regiment Killed in Action

Lt. *Bolesław Jan Rzępołuch*
Corp. *Franciszek Szymański*
Platoon Leader *Jan Pająkowski* U
łan *Ignacy Arszyński*
Ułan Jan Czajkowski
Ułan *Władysław Figielski*
Ułan *Antoni Pietras*
Ułan *Aleksander Sabiniarz*
Ułan *Stefan Sarnowski*
Ułan *Marian Karniewski*
Ułan *Jan Mitag*
Ułan *Wacław Myklikowski*
Ułan *Andrzej Niemiec*
Ułan *Bernard Strzelecki*
Ułan *Edmund Taniłowski*
Ułan *Kazimierz Trojanowski*

The squadrons of the 18th Pomeranian Lancers were deployed on patrol duty until 22 October 1920, when the regiment moved to the area of ***Romanowo***. On 24 October, the 3rd squadron was deployed with the 16th Polish Infantry Division.

The remainder of the regiment eventually left for *Łuniniec* and there, on the axis formed between *Hancewicze* and *Łuniniec*, had the difficult task of patrolling a 200-kilometer area in freezing temperatures as the winter set-in. Matters were made more difficult by the lack of suitable feed for the horses. *Jerzy* received a promotion to Second Lieutenant in December that same year.

In the middle of January 1921, the regiment was transported by rail to *Horodzieje* and, as part of the 5th Mounted Brigade was stationed in the town of *Mir* under the command of Col. *Sochaczewski*. It was given responsibility for patrolling a section of the border by the ***Niemen*** River. The regiment was billeted at *Jeremicze*, with the 1st squadron accommodated at *Wilcze Błoto*, the 2nd squadron at *Pogorełka* and the 3rd squadron at *Mała Obryna*. The 4th squadron remained in *Bołtuny* and the machine guns in *Wielka Obryna*. From mid-January 1921, the troopers of the 18th Pomeranian Lancers occupied the town of *Mir* and for the rest of the winter patrolled the armistice line that had been proposed as the future Polish-Russian border. The regiment would remain there until 1 May 1921.

On 5 May 1921, at the end of a ten-month tour of duty, the regiment returned to its garrison in ***Toruń*** before later being transferred to ***Grudziądz***.

Train, loaded with Polish troops and equipment, waiting to move in one of the Polish or Ukrainian railway stations.

From the Imperial War Museum Collection of images of The Polish-Russian War 1919-1921
Image supplied under license © Imperial War Museum (Q92243) LIC-15996-V8Q5B9

Troops of the Polish transport column feeding their horses in one of the villages.

From the Imperial War Museum Collection of images of The Polish-Russian War 1919-1921
Image supplied under license © Imperial War Museum (Q92236) LIC-15996-V8Q5B9

CHAPTER 7
CAVALRY TRAINING
(1921-1938)

A red two-storey building just inside the gates to the ancient fort at *Grudziądz* was taken over as the 18th Pomeranian Lancers' regimental head-quarters. Numbered 'Hall 1' and 'Hall 2', and subsequently converted for use as military workshops, in 1921 two huge hangars were converted for use as indoor riding schools. A parade ground was cleared for assemblies, regimental parades, drill-practice and other unit-exercises. Inside the regimental barracks there was an officers' mess, an NCOs' mess, troopers' living quarters, an infirmary, a regimental store with a room set aside for refreshments and a library. The citadel had its own fire station, squadron stables and forage store; a stable was converted for use for the treatment of sick, injured or lame horses. Other facilities included a veterinary ambulance, a gunsmith, a detention center, a barber's shop and general workshops. Amenities even extended to a forge, a bakery and a flour mill. Weapon and ammunition stores were located beyond the barracks. Every year, an assessment would be made of the performance of each regiment of Polish cavalry – facilitated by an inter-regiment competition. A '*bunchuk*' (traditionally, a horse tail attached to a pole and used as a symbol of a Hetman's power and a custom brought to Poland from Turkey), was presented to the best squadron. Troopers from the 18th Pomeranian Lancers (2nd Squadron) commanded by Cavalry Capt. *Bolesław Emich* won this coveted trophy in 1933.

Service with the regiment bestowed on each cavalryman three primary obligations: Care for his horse, maintenance of personal-issue weapons and upholding the good name and reputation of the regiment. These duties were underpinned by a rigorously maintained daily routine:

- 0530 - 0600 - Reveille, dress, square away bedding.

- 0600 – 0700 - Stable maintenance (watering, cleaning and feeding of horses).

- 0700 - 0745 - Ablutions, breakfast and preparation for exercise.

- 0745 - 0800 - Kit inspection.

- 0800 - 0845 - Gymnastics or schooling of horses.

- 0845 - 0900 - Saddling horses.

- 0900 - 1030 - Riding or other equestrian drills (once a week, from 0815 to 1045, mounted combat exercises).

- 1030 - 1200 – Attending to horses (cleaning, feeding and watering horses (at the same time, individual target practice exer cises for those selected)).

Twice a month (for 4 hours) artillery practice took place on nearby ranges. On those days, there was no horse-riding and no afternoon classes in field-craft as this time was used for attending to horses.

- 1200 - 1400 - Meal break.

- 1400 - 1700 - Classroom studies. (Twice a week the subjects covered included regimental regulations, guard duty and Polish studies. Three times a week, this period was devoted to firearms training, tactical training and to foot drill).

- 1700 - 1730 - Break.

- 1730 - 1830 - Attending to horses.

- 1830 - 1900 - Evening meal.

- 1900 - 2000 - Free time.

- 2000 - 2030 - Uniform maintenance.

- 2030 - 2045 - Familiarization with following day's orders.

- 2045 - Ablutions and lights out.

Saturday afternoons in the barracks were devoted to ablutions (bathing, laundry etc.). Following completion of a whole week's service, on Sundays and holidays the soldiers were offered a pass and were permitted to remain beyond the confines of the barracks until midnight. Without a pass, absence from barracks was only allowed between 1400 and 1800.

Depending upon the season, the regiment would hold a variety of activities and exercises. From March, mounted and infantry field-combat exercises were organized. Between April and November, mounted and infantry exercises were conducted by the regiment as a whole. Starting in June, the regiment underwent swimming exercises and would leave the garrison for maneuvers lasting several weeks.

Every year the regiment would take possession of approximately forty, 3-year-old horses purchased by a specially-convened committee, that were trained by the reserve squadron. The programme of training lasted for two years prior to allocation of horses to the other squadrons. Each of the squadrons would be assigned horses of a particular color:

- 1st squadron - Maroon chestnut.

- 2nd squadron - Light bay.

- 3rd squadron - Dark bay.

- 4th squadron - Brown bay.

- Heavy machine gun squadron - Black.

- Signal platoon - Chestnut.

- Anti-tank platoon - Roan and slate blue grey.

- Trumpeters' platoon - Grey and slate blue grey.

In August 1921, *Jerzy* was sent for officer training at the Cavalry Training Centre, also located in **Grudziądz**. During this period, he was promoted to 1st Lieutenant and spent the next two years on the Riding Instructors' Course, followed by a short period of assignment to the Cavalry Officer School, as an Instructor.

On 29 May 1923 in **Toruń**, the regiment Commander – Lt. Col. *Stefan Dembiński* was presented with a regimental standard by the President of Poland, *Stanisław Wojciechowski*. The Colors were a symbol of loyalty to the homeland, a symbol of honor and courage. One side of the standard included the emblem of the Polish white eagle, and the other a representation of the Holy Mother of *Częstochowa*, together with the initials of the 18th Pomeranian Lancers Regiment.

The Standard also bore the following inscriptions:

1) 'Pomerania to its Sons'
2) 'President of Poland *Stanisław Wojciechowski*'
3) 'Marshal of Poland *Józef Piłsudski*'
4) 'Minister of Military Affairs, Div. Gen. *Kazimierz Sosnkowski*'
5) 'Lt. Gen. *Tadeusz Rozwadowski*, Inspector General of Cavalry'

The creation of the standard of the 18th Pomeranian Lancers Regiment was funded by the Pomeranian community, following an initiative of Mrs *Maria Czarlińska*, wife of *Adam*, a reserve officer of the unit. The couple were later given the privilege of being honorary guardians to the standard.

The first trooper to formally carry the standard on parade was Sgt *Leon Ciesielski*. On this occasion the Escort to the Color comprised an officer, an additional, younger distinguished non- commissioned officer and three troopers.

In 1924, Lt. Col. *Stefan Dembiński* issued an order for the commissioning of regimental insignia to be worn by officers of the 18th Pomeranian Lancers. Lieutenant *Marian Hernik* proposed a design, later to be officially recognized and catalogued in the *Military Command Journal*, under an entry dated April 1925. The insignia depicted a silver Maltese cross, shaped in the form of the cross of the Polish Order of Virtuti Militari, made from oxidized silver and measuring 44 mm x 44 mm. The cross issued to officers, was covered with a layer of sky blue enamel. In the middle of the cross was the Pomeranian Dragon, astride the letter 'U' on the lower arm of the cross, with the number 18 inside it. A similar cross worn by non-commissioned officers was not coated in enamel. On the rear of each cross was a sequential number.

In order to be eligible for a commemorative cross, soldiers were required to have served with the regiment at the Front for 6 months or more, otherwise to have served with the regiment for at least 12 months. In peacetime, eligibility rose to service with the regiment for a minimum period of two years. Non-military personnel were also eligible to receive a badge in recognition of services rendered to the regiment. The first officer to preside over the committee awarding the regimental badge was Cavalry Capt. *Kazimierz Prandota-Trzciński*.

Crosses were manufactured by *Wiktor Gontarczyk* from Warsaw.

Insignia of the 18ᵗʰ Polish Pomeranian Lancers Regiment
(Image reproduced by kind permission of Sławomir Ziętarski © Sławomir Ziętarski)

In 1924, *Jerzy* returned to operational duty with his regiment. Becoming Regimental, his posting lasted for three years until 1927.

On 19 February 1927, *Jerzy* lost his father *Stefan*, who died peacefully at home in **Radostów**.

During the same year, *Jerzy* was transferred to the Central Cavalry Training School, where he remained for the following five years as an instructor.

Having returned to operational duty with his regiment in **Grudziądz** in 1932, *Jerzy* took up command of a squadron.

On 13 November 1932, *Jerzy* married Countess *Maria Breza*, one of four daughters from a Polish family that can trace its ancestry to the 10th century. Prior to her introduction to *Jerzy*, *Maria* had lived with her aunt, *Konstancja Szułdrzyńska* at the palace of *Sierniki*, near **Poznań**. *Maria* had grown-up there with her three sisters, following the loss of their mother to tuberculosis in 1913. Over time, *Jerzy* would come to rely heavily on the ingenuity and connections that would be forged by *Maria's* sister – *Gabriela*, (better known as *'Soeur Cyrille'* or simply *'Benia'* to the family) and a nun since 1926 with the *Order of Soeurs du Saint-Enfant Jésus* in France.

A year later, *Jerzy* and *Maria* would have their first child, *Theresa*.

Jerzy's mother, *Konstancja*, died on 30 November 1933.

Between 1934 and 1935, *Jerzy* was attached to the Brigade Headquarters as a Staff Officer. Whilst posted to **Białystok** in eastern Poland, *Jerzy* and *Maria* had their second daughter, *Anna* (*"Anita"*) in 1935. They had wanted to call their daughter Anita but the church insisted on her being christened after a saint. There being no Saint 'Anita' at the time, she was duly christened 'Anna', although this latter name only appears on old family documents and she was called "Anita" for the whole of her life.

The following year, as Deputy Squadron Leader, *Jerzy* transferred to the Reserve Squadron of the 18th Polish Pomeranian Lancers in **Toruń**.

In 1936, *Maria* had their third child, a son, *Konstanty* (later known as 'Andy') who was born in **Warsaw**.

W Y C I Ą G

z rozkazu D.O.K.VIII.Nr.50/28. pkt.1.i 2.oraz z załącznika
do rozkazu D.O.K.VIII.Nr.50.pkt.1.i 2.

1.Dział personalny.

1.Medal Pamiątkowy za wojnę 1918 - 1921 r.

17408/Og:pers.Na podstawie rozporządzenia Pana Ministra
Spraw Wojskowych L.30850/B.P.1.z dnia 21.października 1928 r.
przyznaję prawo do medalu Pamiątkowego za wojnę 1918 -1921
/załącznik.

2.Nadanie Medalu"Dziesięciolecia Odzyskanej Niepodległości"

18360/Og:pers.Na podstawie rozporządzenia Pana Ministra
Spraw Wojsk.z dnia 3 listopada 1928 r.ogłaszam jako załącznik
spis osób wojskowych i cywilnych,którym nadaję Medal"Dziesięcio
lecia Odzyskanej Niepodległości".-

Nadanie Medalu Pamiątkowego za wojnę 1918-1921 r.

D.
por.Dobieckiemu Jerzemu - 18.pułk ułanów.

Nadanie Medalu Dziesięciolecia Odzyskanej Niepodległości

P-o-r-u-c-z-n-i-c-y

Dobiecki Józef - 18.pułk ułanów.

zgodność wyciągu   Dowódca Okr.Korp.Nr.VIII.
Adjutant 18.pułku ułanów.   /-/ Stefan Pasławski
                                          generał brygady.

i c h rotm.

18th Polish Pomeranian Lancers Regimental documentation detailing awards in 1928 to Lt.
Jerzy Dobiecki:

1. 1918-1921 War Medal and
2. Medal commemorating 10 years of independence

Jerzy during training as an instructor,
Cavalry Training School, Poland c1930

Jerzy Dobiecki, Poland c1930

W Y C I Ą G

z rozkazu D.O.K. VIII.Nr.50/28. pkt.1.i 2.oraz z załącznika
do rozkazu D.O.K.VIII.Nr.50.pkt.1.i 2.

1.Dział personalny.

1.Medal Pamiątkowy za wojnę 1918 - 1921 r.

17408/Og:pers:Na podstawie rozporządzenia Pana Ministra
Spraw Wojskowych L.30850/B.P.1.z dnia 21.października 1928 r.
przyznaję prawo do medalu Pamiątkowego za wojnę 1918 -1921
/załącznik.

2.Nadanie Medalu"Dziesięciolecia Odzyskanej Niepodległości"

18360/Og:pers:Na podstawie rozporządzenia Pana Ministra
Spraw Wojsk.z dnia 3.listopada 1928 r.ogłaszam jako załącznik
spis osób wojskowych i cywilnych ,którym nadaję Medal"Dziesięcio
lecia Odzyskanej Niepodległości".-

Nadanie Medalu Pamiątkowego za wojnę 1918-1921 r.

D.
por.Dobieckiemu Jerzemu - 18.pułk ułanów.

Nadanie Medalu Dziesięciolecia Odzyskanej Niepodległości

P o r u c z n i c y

Dobiecki Józef ,- 18.pułk ułanów.

zgodność wyciągu
Adjutant 18. pułku ułanów.   Dowódca Okr.Korp.Nr.VIII.
                                              /-/ Stefan Paskawski
                                                  generał brygady.
ich rotm.

Military Transfer Notices, Cavalry Training Centre *Grudziądz*, Poland, 1932
The notice reads:

"...By order of the Ministry of Military Affairs, Personnel Department, No. 3110-105/Kaw.32, the following transfers of personnel are announced:

3)   *Lieut. Dobiecki Jerzy – to the 18th Ułan Regiment..."*

"...On behalf of the service, I express my gratitude for his contribution over the past 4-years to the work of the Cavalry Training Centre and wish him further good fortune during his next posting with his parent regiment – the 18th Pomeranian Ułans - a regiment that has such close links, on so many levels, with this training establishment...".

Jerzy with officers of the 18th Polish Pomeranian Lancers, Poland c1932
(from the private collection of *Sławomir Ziętarski* ©Sławomir Ziętarski)

(Left to Right)

Front row:
Maj. *Jan Ciechanowicz*, Maj. *Marian Ossowski*, Col. *Albert Traeger*, Maj. *Stefan Platonoff*, Lt. *Janusz Łoś*, Lt. *Leonard Fijałkowski*, 2nd Lt. *Józef Karczewski*.

Second Row:
Capt. *Władysław Niegowski*, Lt. *Szymon Kabiaszwili*, Lt. *Marceli Wos*.

Third Row:
Capt. *Bolesław Emlich*, Capt. *Wacław Jastrzębski*, Lt. *Janusz Skarbek Tłuchowski*, Capt. *Ryszard Stanisław Lewicki*.

Fourth Row:
Lt. *Jerzy Dobiecki*, Lt. *Janusz Kierzkowski*, Lt. *Wacław Godlewski*, Lt. *Tadeusz Łoś*, Capt. *Sławomir Gabriel De Latur*.

Fifth Row:
Lt. *Józef Turkowski*, Lt. *Włodzimierz Raczyński*, Lt. *Eugeniusz Świeściak*, Lt. *Włodzimierz Sokulski*, Lt. *Jan Ładoś*, Lt. *Henryk Odyniec Dobrowolski*, Lt. *Rudolf Hołdun - Płatnik*
(Listing provided by Andrzej Szutowicz)

Jerzy with his brothers (left to right) *Stanisław, Jerzy* and *Kazimierz Dobiecki*,
Poland c1932

Palace of *Sierniki*, (home of the *Szułdrzyński* family)
Near *Poznań*, Poland c1930

Jerzy's father and mother-in-law, Count *Stanisław* and Countess *Maria* BREZA,
Poland early 1900s

A photograph from Maria Breza's early life (left to right)
Stanisław Borowski, Marian Szułdrzyński, Andrzej Szułdrzyński, Anusia Szułdrzyńska, Anna Breza, Zula Szułdrzyńska, Zofia Breza, Maria Breza (Jerzy's future wife), *Gabriela Breza*

Switzerland 1914

Jerzy Dobiecki with his father-in-law, Count *Stanisław Breza* and wife, *Maria Breza*
Poland c1932

Maria with *Jerzy Dobiecki*, Poland c1932

(left to right)
Jerzy and *Maria Dobiecki* (holding daughter *Theresa* (my mother)) with *Maria's* sisters, *Zofia* and *Anna Breza*, Poland, 1933

(left to right)
Daughters *Theresa* and *Anna* ("Anita") with *Jerzy*
Poland c1938

Ian von Heintze

CHAPTER 8
THE SECOND WORLD WAR (1939-1945)
(Including a translation of *Jerzy's* personal war diary)

Between 1936 and the outbreak of the Second World War in September 1939, Jerzy was posted to the Ministry of Military Affairs in **Warsaw** (referred-to by the family as the '*Gabinet Główny*'). Today the office is known as the Ministry of National Defense. On 19 March 1937 he was promoted to the rank of Cavalry Captain ('*Rotmistrz*') and was attached as an Aide to the Political Office of the Minister, Div. Gen. *Tadeusz Kasprzycki*.

On the eve of the invasion of Poland by Germany, *Jerzy, Maria* and the children were staying at their apartment in **Warsaw**. When he bid farewell to the family on the morning of 1 September 1939, Jerzy would not be reunited with them again until 1947 – eight years later.

On the first day of the Second World War, *Jerzy* was on liaison duties in Warsaw, accompanying a film crew that was being given a conducted tour of the capital's defenses and filming the preparations being made for war.

Elsewhere in Poland, *Jerzy's* regiment – the 18th Polish Pomeranian Lancers, was already close to being fully mobilized when the German attacks on Poland came.

At 4.45 a.m. on 1 September 1939, German forces began their invasion of Poland. Broadly, the German attack came on four fronts – from the north, the north-west, the west and crossing into Poland additionally from the south. Under the command of Col. *Kazimierz Mastalerz*, the regiment was deployed with a number of others as a part of the Pomeranian Cavalry Brigade (its headquarters located at the common school building in *Czersk*) commanded by Gen. *Stanisław Grzmot-Skotnicki*. The brigade formed part of Poland's 'Army *Pomorze*' – the country's land forces having been previously divided into seven 'Armies' (see Appendix 4(A)). The Pomeranian Cavalry Brigade, including the 18th Pomeranian Lancers had orders to protect the northern and southerly flanks of the defenses at *Chojnice* (north-west of **Toruń**). Under this plan the brigade was to provide cover for the retreat of other units of the Polish army that were in a tactical withdrawal from superior numbers of German forces, rapidly sweeping north to south through what was known as the 'Pomeranian corridor'. The brigade was providing a defensive front between *Moszenica – Lichnowy – Gronowo – Sternowo – Rytel* and along a position extending between *Angowice – Lichnowy – Pawłowo, Szenfeld – Dręgowice – Angowice – Nowy Dwór*.

During the late afternoon and early evening of 1 September, units of the 18th Polish Pomeranian Lancers Regiment had been moving under cover of dense forest, close to the village of **Krojanty** (to the north of **Bydgoszcz** in northern Poland). The Polish Lancers came into contact with troops of the 76th

Motorized German Infantry. The German unit was led by Lt. Gen. *Mauritz von Wiktorin* and was part of the 20th German motorized Infantry Division, commanded by Gen. *Heinz Guderian*. The German forces had been previously engaging the Polish army in the *Tuchola* forest and through the course of the day, despite having been repulsed in several earlier attacks, were now pushing the Poles back. Still in full daylight and under cover of the forest, the units of the 18th Pomeranian Lancers could observe the enemy maneuvering in a clearing. Colonel *Mastalerz* gave orders to his two mounted squadrons of Lancers to attack the rear of the, now exposed, flank of the German unit. The first squadron slowly advanced under the command of Cavalry Capt. *Eugeniusz Świeściak*, to be joined on its right by the 2nd squadron, led by Cavalry Capt. *Jan Ładoś*. The retinue of the commander – Col. *Mastalerz*, followed towards the rear. The mounted units of the 18th Pomeranian Lancers, using the dense tree-line as cover, both fanned-out towards the German troops. At the last possible moment and on reaching the edge of the forest, the Lancers drew their sabers and charged into the open clearing towards the unsuspecting German infantry. Within a very short space of time, the two squadrons were able to inflict a number of casualties[1]. According to *Zygfryd Szych*, who was to make several later visits to the site of the engagement after the war, accompanied by former Ułans of the 18th Pomeranian Regiment[2], the charge lasted about one and a half minutes.

The advantage was however, short-lived. Unexpectedly and to the left of the charging Polish horsemen, a column of German armored cars, previously also hidden by the forest, suddenly appeared and bore down on the cavalry unit – laying down heavy fire as they advanced. This action would prove to be devastating and inflicted immediate casualties on the unprotected Polish cavalry. The troopers of the 18th Pomeranian Lancers did what they could to hastily withdraw and to regroup close to a nearby embankment, forced to leave the dead and injured where they lay.

Heavy losses were suffered by the 1st squadron and the battalion as a whole lost much of its strength. Amongst the first to fall was Cavalry Capt. *Świeściak*. The regiment commander's retinue was cut-down by the machine-gun fire. Colonel *Kazimierz Mastalerz* and 2nd Lt. *Tadeusz Milicki* were also killed.

The following day, Italian war-correspondents sent to report from the scene, were given a factually incorrect account of what had occurred in the forest near **Krojanty** the previous day. German soldiers went on record stating that the mounted troopers of the 18th Polish Pomeranian Lancers had been killed whilst mounting a fruitless cavalry charge against German tanks, a charge that was doomed to failure from the start. This story, intended to bolster German propaganda and to highlight the futility of any resistance to the might of the German army, was widely reported at the time and embellished by the Nazis as time wore on.[3] The misreported charge by Polish cavalry on

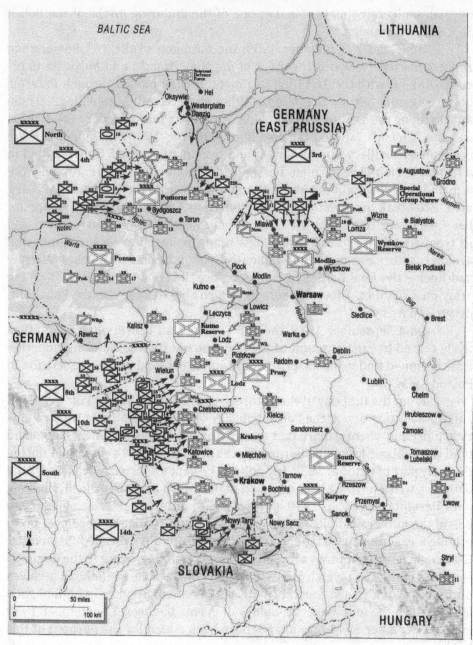

The German Attack on Poland, 1 September 1939
(© Osprey Publishing Group)
(Reproduced by kind permission of Osprey Publishing)

German tanks remains to this day, one of the enduring myths of the Polish September Campaign.

On 2 and 3 September 1939, the battalion of the 18th Pomeranian Lancers marched towards the areas of *Błądzim, Bramka* and *Bukowiec* in order to link-up with the 16th Ułan Regiment. Having passed through *Drzecim*, both regiments left for **Grudziądz**. Although successfully repelling German attacks along the way, whilst marching as part of a rear-guard for the 1st Rifle and the *"Czersk"* National Defense Battalions, the 18th Pomeranian Lancers came under artillery bombardment and became disbursed. This resulted in a further serious loss of men, horses and equipment. After regrouping, the remainder of the regiment started to march towards the Vistula river. Being unable to break through German positions to get to **Grudziądz**, on 4 September - what was left of the 18th Pomeranian Regiment, was surrounded and its troopers taken prisoner. Only a few Ułans managed to escape. Those that avoided capture escaped to subsequently fight in the battles of Bzura, Warsaw and Kock – the final battles in Poland before the country fell to the German army on 3 October. A few troopers were also able to later join the Polish Underground Army.

On 4 September 1939, the 18th Pomeranian Lancers Regiment effectively ceased to exist as a unit of the Polish Army. Its traditions are nonetheless continued under the auspices of the volunteer Regimental Association in Poland today.

From the first day of the outbreak of the Second World War in Poland and from his position at the Polish Ministry of Military Affairs in Warsaw, Jerzy kept a hand-written diary that records the military deployments in Poland until the final battle against German forces prior to Poland's surrender during the early part of October 1939. In addition, he kept a shorter, much less formal daily-log, written whilst later attached to the Polish Army in exile in Scotland, until December 1944. In 1940, in response to orders to provide evidence to one of the numerous Polish Commissions of Enquiry that had been set-up to establish exactly what happened in Poland during the so-called 'September Campaign', *Jerzy* submitted a formal statement as his evidence to the Commission. The diary upon which *Jerzy's* statement was based, confined to archives until now, when joined together with his personal, previously unpublished log, provides the following chronology of events between 1 September 1939 and 23 December 1944 (the images have been added for the purpose of this book):

EXTRACT FROM JERZY'S WAR DIARY[4]

29th July 1939

I am assigned to the Anglo-American film crew, making a Polish-English propaganda film. I am accompanied by Douglas Slocombe and

Herbert Kline – with their wives.

30ᵗʰ July 1939

*We film scenes of mobilization and anti-aircraft defenses of **Warsaw**.*

1ˢᵗ August 1939

*At 8.00 a.m., together with other staff from the Ministry, we leave **Warsaw** from the Main Railway Station – signs of the first air raids – you can hear explosions towards **Toruń**. Our train is bombarded as we arrive in **Kutno** at 6.00 p.m. – we have to stay here for the night.*

*Germans cross the Polish border. Attack on **Mława** and **Grudziądz** from East Prussia; from **Gdańsk** on **Gdynia** and Tczew; from German Pomerania on Chojnice and Koronowo; from the area of **Wrocław**/Opole on the line of Wieruszków/**Częstochowa** and Rybnik/Mikołów; from Slovakia in the direction of Chabówka.*

Westerplatte attacked by land and shelled by the battleship Schleswig-Holstein.

*The enemy air force carries out 71 attacks, bombing airports, airstrips, railway junctions and, on two occasions, **Warsaw**. The enemy suffers heavy damage to its artillery.*

2ⁿᵈ September 1939

*At 8 a.m. we depart from **Kutno**. At 12 noon, we arrive in Toruń, where I report to The Corps District Commander, Brigadier General Tokarzewski, who issues me with an order to go the following day to Bydgoszcz and then to **Grudziądz**. We film a shot-down German plane.*

*Fighting continues in positions along the border. Armored units attack from Koronowo. Armored units break to the north of Częstochowa to the Gidle area. Battles of **Mława**, Wieruszów – Wieluń– Działoszyn, Pszczyna, Żywiec, Rabka – Jordanów. The Polish air force bombs German armored units in the Kłobuck area. The German air forces bombs lines of communication, depots, airports and industrial centers.*

3ʳᵈ September 1939

*Due to the action on the Western Front and the failure to obtain a car, instead of going to **Bydgoszcz** and **Grudziądz** we film scenes of anti-aircraft defenses and air raids on **Toruń**. Under instructions from The District Corps Commander, at 6 p.m. we depart towards **Warsaw** through Sierpc.*

*Order issued for the Polish troops to retreat to the axis of the Narew – **Bug** – **Vistula** – **Warta** – Nida – Dunajec rivers. Withdrawal from **Mława** and*

Grudziądz. *The enemy carries out an armored attack on Świecie nad Wisłą, from **Częstochowa** on Kamińsk and Przedbórz and from Chabówka on Mszana. Placing troops in **Częstochowa** and Szczekociny. New attack in the direction of Nowy Sącz. Polish cavalry penetrates into East Prussia. Efficient bombardment of German artillery positions in the areas of Radomsko and Gidle – Pławno. Enemy air force bombing communications, transport and, 6 times, **Warsaw**.*

4ᵗʰ *September 1939*

*Whilst en route – our train is bombed in Nasielsk. Late into the night we eventually pull into **Modlin**.*

*In the morning, the enemy occupies **Bydgoszcz**, after the retreat of our troops. Battle of Maków– Ciechanów and of **Inowrocław**. Occupation of **Chełmno** nad Wisłą. Polish Armies: 'Poznań', 'Łódź' and 'Kraków' retreat to new positions.*

*Occupation of Limanowa and Stary Sącz. Armored units carry out an attack towards Piotrków and on **Kielce**. The Polish air force bombs an armored group to the north of Radomsko and at Ciechanów. The enemy air force sinks the destroyer "Wicher" and the minelayer "Gryf" at **Gdynia**. Destruction of the Inowrocław railway station. Bombing of the Lines: **Kutno – Warsaw, Kraków – Lwów, Kielce – Radom**.*

5ᵗʰ *September 1939*

*From **Modlin**, we hitch a ride on board the locomotive of an armored train that takes us to Legionowo; from here we manage to get to **Warsaw** by train. At 12.00 noon, I report at the Ministry of Military Affairs located at Chocimska Street, to the Head of the Political Office of the Minister of Military Affairs, Colonel Kiliński, who informs me that the Ministry of Military Affairs has been evacuated beyond **Lublin** – employees and families were transported by train yesterday evening. A few of us that remain will leave by car and make our way there in a few hours' time. I receive permission and drop into my flat at Czeczota Street in the Mokotów District for half an hour. I return to the office, from where, at 4 p.m., we depart by car – an off-road Fiat 518: Colonel Kiliński, Captain Kłak, myself and Ensign Zieliński – driver: Fabianowicz.*

*At 9.00 p.m., we arrive in **Lublin**, from where we go to Bystrzejowice near **Wierzchowiska**, where the evacuees were apparently heading.*

*From the direction of East Prussia, motorized units of the enemy have reached the **Narew** River at Różan and Ostrołęka. From **Chełmno**, the enemy advances towards **Toruń**. On the coast, a battle has started between Wejherowo – Sobieszyno and Kołaczkowo – Wiczlino. Fighting between the*

Warta and *Widawka* rivers leads to the occupation of *Sieradz. After seizing Rozprza, an encounter with the reserve army at **Piotrków**.*

*Motorized units reach **Łopuszno** and Chęciny in the direction of **Kielce**. Fighting between Myślenice, Lipnica – Murowana, Bobowa – Gorlice.*

*An order to create the 'Lublin Army' for the defense of the middle **Vistula** River.*

The Polish air force bombs armored columns at Ciechanów and on a road at Różan.

*The enemy air force activity as the day before. Intensive air battles. A long air raid on **Warsaw**.*

6th September 1939

Stopover, Bystrzejowice.

*Crossing of the **Narew** River at Różan. Attack on Pułtusk. Fighting in the Tuchola Forest finishes. Pomeranian ('Pomorze'), 'Poznań' and 'Łódź' Armies receive an order to retreat to the east beyond the **Vistula** River. After the fight at Pułtusk – Chełsty, the 'Narew' group receives an order to retreat to the **Bug** River.*

*The enemy occupies **Kraków**, **Kielce** and Tomaszów Mazowiecki. Battles of Skarżysko, Gorlice, Bochnia and Wiśnicz.*

*The Polish air force bombs the areas of Różan and Piotrków and takes part in air battles against the **Warsaw – Grudziądz** axis.*

*German air force bombs: The East Railway station in **Warsaw**, railway lines of **Lwów – Kraków** and **Kielce – Radom** and the rear flank in the area of the 'Łódź' Army.*

7th September 1939

My brother 'Kazio' (Kazimierz) and I meet up.

*The enemy occupies **Pułtusk**. Armored units occupy Rawa Mazowiecka and fight at Tuszyn. The reserve army retreats to the **Vistula** River. In the South, armored units occupy Dębiec and Jasło. The 'Kraków' Army retreats beyond the **Vistula** and **San** rivers and the 'Karpaty' Army retreats to the Wisłok River.*

*The Polish air force bombs enemy columns on the roads **Łódź** – Łęczyca and Różan – Ostrołęka. The German air force bombs railway stations and bridges on the **Bug** and **Vistula** rivers.*

8ᵗʰ *September 1939*

*The Ministry of Military Affairs is evacuated further back to Łuck in order to be able to work undisrupted. Colonel Kiliński, acting as a messenger between the Minister and the Commander-in-Chief, accompanies me to **Brześć nad Bugiem.** Heavy bombing. General Bałachowicz, General Skierski, General Ładoś are organizing defense forces. On receiving information that a German motorized group is approaching Wysokie Litewskie (Vysokaye) from the north – about 30 km from Brześć, at 7.00 p.m. orders are issued for the High Command to move to **Włodzimierz** Wołyński (**Volodymyr-Volynskyi**) under cover of darkness. When we depart, along the way we witness burning villages and a sawmill on fire by the station in Włodawa.*

*Skirmishes between the **Narew** River, **Łomża** – Ostrowiec and in the area of Ostrów Mazowiecka, armored units occupy Mszczonów, reach the outskirts of **Warsaw**, place troops in **Radom** from where they head north and south. From **Kielce**, they reach Staszów. In the south, Rzeszów and **Krosno** are occupied. By the order of the Polish High Command, **Westerplatte** surrenders. Fighting in the defense of **Gdynia** and the Oksywie naval bases.*

*The Polish High Command issues an order to defend the **Bug, Vistula** and **San** rivers and for the 'Poznań' and 'Pomorze' Armies to attack **Łódź** and **Radom**. During the day, four bombings of German armored units.*

*Germans bomb bridges on the **Vistula** and **Bug** rivers, as well as towns and roads leading to the **Vistula** and **San** rivers.*

9ᵗʰ *September 1939*

Armored units attack **Łomża** and Wizna, as well as Wyszków. Placing troops in **Łódź** on the outskirts of **Warsaw** /Grójec, Nadarzyn. Fighting at Maciejowice and Iłża. Motorized armored units reach the **Vistula** River at **Sandomierz**. Fighting at Łańcut, Przeworskand Sanok. An armored unit reaches **Jaworsko** Polskie. Fighting at Połaniec and Oleśnica – Staszów area.

The Polish air force bombs the Małkinia area. Major air battles over Rawa, **Radom, Kielce** and the **San** River.

Intensive German bombing of towns and roads to the East of the **Vistula** River, with a special focus on Praga, a suburb of **Warsaw** on the east bank of the **Vistula** River and roads between Lwów (L'viv) and **San**, as well as bridges on the **San** River.

10ᵗʰ *September 1939*

*Battle of Zambrów, in the area to the east of Ostrów Mazowiecka and Brok. Crossing of the **Bug** River at Wyszków. Fighting at Okęcie and in the Skier-*

niewice area, Słupia and Łyszkowice. Polish attack from Łęczyca. Fighting in the direction of Radymno and Chyrów. Breaking through the defense line of **Gdynia** *and occupation of Wejherowo. The Polish High Command issues an order to retreat to the area of Polesie and the* **Wieprz, Vistula** *and* **San** *rivers. The enemy air force bombs larger towns to the east of the* **Vistula** *River, with a focus on the roads leading from Praga, as well as the* **Lwów** *area.*

11th September 1939

I am handed my salary for October and November from the Political Office of the Minister of 1,280 złoty.

Armored units attack from the Zambrów area in the direction of **Białystok**, *Siemiatycze and from Małkinia on Siedlce – Kałuszyn.*

During a night attack, a group of German tanks is destroyed at Kałuszyn. Attack from Wyszków towards **Warsaw** *and Mińsk Mazowiecki. German defense between Pardubice, Żartków, Głowno, Bielawa, Łowicz. A battle in the area of Żyrardów, Pruszków, Brwinów and Baranów nad Wisłą. A further Polish attack on* **Łódź** *extended by an attack on Skierniewice and occupation of Łowicz. The enemy reaches the* **Vistula** *bank from* **Radom** *to* **Sandomierz**. *Occupation of* **Kraków** *and Chyrów. – Siege of the Oksywie naval base, occupation of Puck, Wielka Wieś – Hallerowo.*

The Polish air force bombs crossings at Radymno and the Jarosław area. The German air force bombs the area of the roads – **Kutno**, *Łowicz, Gostyń, Gostynice. A number of larger towns, especially* **Lwów, Lublin, Chełm**, *Łuków.*

12th September 1939

At 2.00 a.m., via **Chełm** *and* **Hrubieszów**, *we arrive in Włodzimierz Wołyński.*

Germans attack Ossowiec and armored units reach Wysokie Litewskie and Siemiatycze. Kałuszyn is reached, as is **Wyszogród** *on the* **Vistula** *River. The enemy's motorized units cross the* **Vistula** *River at Annopol. Armored units occupy Jaworów and from Chyrów they reach* **Lwów**. *The Polish air force bombs the Rawa Ruska area. Long bombing of Oksywie by the Luftwaffe.* **Białystok**, *Kowel and Włodzimierz railway stations are destroyed.*

13th September 1939

Stopover. The Minister arrives from Łuck.

In Łuck, Bishop Gawlina is injured by bomb shrapnel and his chaplain, Rev. Drużbacki, is killed.

*Further push towards **Brześć**, Siedlce, Łuków and **Warsaw**. Occupation of Ossowiec. Battle of Dęby Wielkie involving Polish cavalry.*

*Fight of a motorized German unit at Annopol and crossing of the **Vistula** River at **Dęblin**. Fighting between Ozorków and Łowicz. Gen. Kurzeba decides to regroup for the attack on **Warsaw**. A motorized unit occupies Rawa Ruska.*

*Polish bombers attack armored columns at Rawa Ruska and the **Tomaszów Lubelski** – Rawa Ruska road.*

*The German air force burns Siedlce, Biała Podlaska and Krystynopol, bombs roads between the **Vistula** and **Bug** rivers, the area of **Kutno** and Łuck – Dubno.*

14<u>th</u> September 1939

*Grman motorized groups approach **Zamość**. At 1 a.m. we receive an order that the High Command should move further south. At 2 a.m. we leave and pass through the following towns: Młynów, Dubno, Krzemieniec, Zbaraż, **Tarnopol**, Trembowla, Kopyczyńce, Czortków to Horodenka.*

*German troops get to **Brześć** and **Prużany**, reaching the **Vistula** River from **Modlin** to Praga, where the fighting takes place. A battle from **Kutno**, along the Bzura River, to Łowicz and Sochaczew. Motorized units attack Kraśnik. **Tomaszów** is occupied from the side of Rawa Ruska. Fighting in forests near Biłgoraj. Sambor is occupied. Destruction of an armored German unit by a strong attack near Jaworowo, Nowosiółki, Mażyłowice, Mogiłki.*

Activity of the air force reaches the Soviet border with planes flying in loose formations.

15<u>th</u> September 1939

*We arrive in Kołomyja (**Kolomyia**).*

*Germans occupy **Białystok**, surround the **Brześć** Citadel and push towards Łuków and **Dęblin**.*

*Fighting at Sochaczew. Battle of Cieszanów, Tarnogród and Biłgoraj. Motorized units positioned in **Zamość**. An order of the Polish High Command to create a defense outpost of Dniestr – Sryj. The Polish air force bombs roads near **Hrubieszów**.*

*The German air force bombs, among others, the station in Baranowicze and **Mława**.*

16th September 1939

Stopover in Kołomyja.

German troops position themselves between the Biebrza River and **Brześć,** *advance and occupy Biała Podlaska, Łuków and* **Dęblin.** *Polish attack on Warsaw by the 'Poznań' Army leads to the crossing of the Bzura River and a part of this Army enters* **Warsaw.** *A tough battle at Sochaczew. Fighting near Lublin, Biłgoraj, on the Tanew River. At* **Lwów,** *a Polish attack on Zboiska and on Brzuchowice from Janów. Germans occupy* **Przemyśl** *and retain Sambor. Near Włodawa, a motorized unit from* **Brześć** *encounters a motorized unit advancing from the south through* **Chełm.**
(Continued...)

On 17 September 1939, Soviet troops entered Poland to occupy the Eastern half of the country, in accordance with a previous Soviet pact with Germany. The Polish Commander-in-Chief (Marshal *Eduard Rydz-Śmigły*) had been ordering the repeated withdrawal of Polish troops in a south-easterly direction across Poland in the face of the German army's advance, anticipating the imminent support from Poland's allies – Britain and France. In a surprise move and double blow to the Poles, when Russian forces crossed into Poland from the east, this put the Polish army in an impossible position. In the absence of the expected assistance from her allies, Poland was totally overwhelmed by both the German and Soviet offensives. Instead of surrendering to either German or Soviet commanders on the ground, and in order to keep intact as much of the Polish army that remained to ensure a continuation of the fight from beyond Poland's borders, the Polish government, Military High Command and components of the army crossed the border into Romania and Hungary on 18 September 1939. At the same time, all military personnel that could were ordered to make for this border.

Political pressure was now brought to bear on the Romanian authorities by the German government in regard to the Poles fleeing into Romania on 18 September. The Poles – including *Jerzy*, were arrested and placed into detention centers for allegedly breaching Romanian immigration formalities. Nonetheless, over the following months many of the Poles were able to escape and to find ways of crossing Europe to France or to flee in the direction of Spain, Africa and the Middle East.

On 12 December 1939, *Jerzy* slipped away from his holding center in Romania and made his way on foot to Bucharest. Here he was able to secure the help of the Polish diplomatic mission that enabled him to leave Romania posing as a driver and to drive the 3,400 kilometers to France, arriving in Paris sixteen days later.

17th September 1939

We learn that the Bolsheviks have crossed our border into Poland. The High Command moves to Kosów (Kosiv).

*Germans occupy the **Brześć** Citadel. Fighting on the northern line of So-chaczew to **Kutno** which has been occupied by Germans. Another group of the 'Poznań' and 'Pomorze' Armies reaches **Warsaw** and **Modlin. Lwów** surrounded on three sides. Fighting at Włodawa and Sawin near **Chełm**. Battle of Józefów. Polish troops capture Brzuchowice and Rzęsna near **Lwów**.*

18th September 1939

At 2.30 p.m., on the instructions of the Minister – Division General Kasprzycki, together with the entire group of officers and officials from the Political Office of the Minister, we cross the Polish-Romanian border at Kuty. At 2 a.m. arrive in Wyżnica – Romania.

*Germans capture the Oksywie hills. Fighting at **Modlin** and **Warsaw**. A battle with the rear guard of the 'Poznań' and 'Pomorze' Armies in the fork of the Bzura and **Vistula** rivers. Polish attack on **Tomaszów**, Bełżec and Narol.*

19th September 1939

We arrive at Radowicz - Romania.

*Breakthrough of the remaining groups from the rear guard of the 'Poznań' and Pomorze' Armies. Siege of **Modlin, Warsaw** and fighting in the Kampinos Forest. Battle of the Hel Peninsula.*

20th September 1939

Botosani – Romania.

*Battle of Hel. Siege of **Modlin, Warsaw**. Fighting between **Zamość** and **Hrubieszów**. Fighting at **Lwów**.*

21st September 1939

Focsani – Romania

*The Oksywie naval base surrenders. Battles of **Modlin, Warsaw, Lwów** and Hel. Battle of Narol.*

22nd September 1939

Sarat to Braila – Romania.

*Battles of **Zamość** and **Tomaszów**. Polish cavalry captures Suchowola. **Lwów** surrenders to the Soviets. German attack on Praga and the northern* *line of the **Warsaw** defense.*

23ʳᵈ September 1939

Tulcea – Romania. I work in the staff office of the Polish Army Delegation, first at Lieutenant General Berbecki's and after his departure at Colonel Liebich's until 11ᵗʰ October.

*Battles of Hel, **Warsaw** and **Modlin** continue. End of the battles of **Zamość** and **Tomaszów**. The 'Polesie' defense group starts an attack on the **Bug** River.*

24ᵗʰ September 1939

*Battles of **Warsaw, Modlin**, Hel and of a group of Polish troops in the area of **Lublin, Zamość, Tomaszów**.*

25ᵗʰ September 1939

*All-day aerial bombardment of **Warsaw**. Attack on Mokotow, a suburb of **Warsaw**.*

26ᵗʰ September 1939

*Aerial bombardment of **Modlin**. Battle of Nisko.*

27ᵗʰ September 1939

Battle of Biłgoraj. Cavalry fighting at Dobromil and Husaków.

28ᵗʰ September 1939

*Talks of **Warsaw**'s capitulation.*

29ᵗʰ September 1939

Border Protection Corps fighting at Grabowo.

30ᵗʰ September 1939

***Modlin** capitulates. Fighting at Hańsk and Wytyczne.*

1ˢᵗ October 1939

End of fighting at Hańsk.

2ⁿᵈ October 1939

Battle of Kock and to the south of Nisko.

3rd October 1939

End of the battle of Kock.

11th October 1939

With Colonel Liebich and the entire Polish Army camp, we go to Babadag (Romania).

12th/13th November 1939

During the early hours of the morning of 13th November, we burnt two sacks of złoty banknotes, amounting to eight hundred thousand złoty (800,000 złoty).

On the exchange rate, today, 1 złoty equals 20 lei, so for the amount of money we burnt you could buy:

  160 Chevrolet cars;
  400 thousand all-day expense vouchers to the officers' mess;
  4 thousand sets of civilian clothes;
  2 million loaves of bread;
  8 million "Olla" condoms.

1st December 1939

I depart with 22 officers from the Delegation Office. All officers (apart from Col. Liebich and 2 officers) are transported by the Romanians to a camp in Targoviste for not conforming with Romanian regulations. All staff officers from Calimanesti are to be brought there as well.

3rd December 1939

We arrive in Targoviste.

9th December 1939

Staff officers from Calimanesti arrive.

12th December 1939

I flee from Targoviste.

13th December 1939

I arrive in Bucharest, where I attempt to sort out passport formalities etc.

1940

1st January 1940

I visit the Zielińskis to discuss my options. A suggestion to depart by car.

4th January 1940

I depart from Bucharest in a car provided by the Embassy. I pose as the driver of Dr Niekraszewicz. I drive through Ploiesti and Pitesti.

5ᵗʰ January 1940
Targoviste, Slatina, Craiova, Turnu-Severin.

6th January 1940
The Danube, Bazias, Yugoslavia border – Pancevo.

8ᵗʰ January 1940
Beograd (Belgrade).

9ᵗʰ January 1940
Pancevo – Beograd – Osijek.

10ᵗʰ January 1940
Pluj – Ljubljana.

11ᵗʰ January 1940
Ljubljana – Italy border.

12ᵗʰ January 1940
Trieste.

13ᵗʰ January 1940
Venice – Padua.

14ᵗʰ January 1940
Vicenza – Verona, Lake Garda – Milan.

15ᵗʰ January 1940
Milan – Varazze.

16th January 1940
San Remo – Ventimiglia – French border – Menton.

17ᵗʰ January 1940
Menton – Monte Carlo – Nice.

18ᵗʰ January 1940
Nice, Juan les Pins, Cannes, Avignon.

19ᵗʰ January 1940
St. Etienne – Vichy – Moulins.

20ᵗʰ January 1940
Fontainebleau – Paris, I arrive at 3 p.m. From Bucharest, it has taken 16 days and I have travelled 3,400 km.

Via the embassy, I am accommodated at the Grand Hotel de Paris, 24 rue Bonaparte, by the church of St. Germain-des-Prés; Mme Penard
(continued...)

Back in Poland meanwhile, in the void that was left between the advancing Soviet and German fronts in eastern Poland, small groups of bandits from Belarus and Ukraine preyed on sparsely populated, remote rural communes. Although the lawlessness continued well into the war, as Russia took over more territory, the banditry decreased – small comfort to the thousands of Poles who were about to be deported from these areas of eastern Poland to Siberia, in Russia. The majority of those deported were military settlers – families of Polish soldiers who had previously fought with distinction during the war with Russia in 1920, and who had been given land in eastern Poland for their services. In February 1940, 26,790 families (139,286 people in total)[5] were removed to Siberia with three major deportations to Russia occurring after that – amounting to some 1,200,000 Polish civilians being taken from Poland, ostensibly as punishment for their involvement in the war of 1919-1921.

Following Germany's later attack on Russia in June 1941, many of the deported Polish soldiers were actually released under an amnesty by the Russians, to be mustered into a Polish Army on Soviet soil, commanded by Lt. Gen. *Władisław Anders*. However, as the situation in Russia deteriorated, this Polish army was itself evacuated through Iran to Iraq and on to the British-controlled areas of the Middle East.

Despite the deportations from Poland in 1940, many Poles continued to flee south and westwards and a large number of them were able to reach French controlled Syria. The numbers were sufficient for the formation of a Polish unit there as well (the Polish Carpathian Rifle Brigade), under the command of Gen. *Stanisław Kopański*. The unit later crossed into British-ruled Palestine and formed part of several infantry divisions of the Polish 2nd Corps under Gen. *Anders*.

Approximately 80,000 of the Polish servicemen who were able to cross the continent into France, were placed under the orders of the Polish Government that had by then been formed in exile in Paris. The soldiers were organized into a Free Polish Army of motorized brigades and infantry divisions, commanded by Gen. *Władisław Sikorski* – appointed as Polish Prime Minister and Supreme Commander of the Polish Armed Forces. Some of the training of the Polish troops arriving in France took place in Britany. Many of the Poles were issued with French uniforms and were armed with French rifles. The Poles subsequently sent a detachment to Norway (the Independent Polish Highland brigade, commanded by Gen. *Zygmunt Szyszko-Bohusz*), which was to later return to support French troops in the defense of France.

Whilst in France, *Jerzy* was given a role in the communications and postal department at the Polish embassy in Paris and for a short while he acted as liaison officer between the embassy and the Paris central Post office. As Paris fell to German forces the following year in June 1940, the Allied forces were made to retreat to the northern coast of France. Those units of the Free Polish Forces that were not taken captive by the Germans, made their way across France to seek evacuation from the French Atlantic ports (*Cherbourg, St Malo, Brest, St Nazaire, La Rochelle, La Pallice, Le Verdon, Bordeaux, St Jan de Luz and Marseilles*). The Polish Government that had set itself up in France meanwhile, moved temporarily to *Angers* before transferring to London. On 10th June, *Jerzy* re-located to *Chemille* near *Angers*, having been given custody

*Jerzy Dobiecki, **Budapest** 1939*

Polish ten złoty note with Jerzy's remarks:

"....... *During the early hours of the morning of 13th November, we burnt two sacks of złoty banknotes, amounting to eight hundred thousand złoty (800,000 złoty).*
On the exchange rate, today, 1 złoty equals 20 lei, so for the amount of money we burnt you could buy:
160 Chevrolet cars;
400 thousand all-day expense vouchers to the officers' mess; 4 thousand sets of civilian clothes;
2 million loaves of bread;
8 million "Olla" condoms......."

of a quantity of sensitive Polish diplomatic documentary material for transport to the safety of Britain. He would now also make his way south to *Bordeaux* on 20th June and together with large numbers of Poles, was transported by ship to England, arriving at Liverpool docks on 25th June 1940.

EXTRACT FROM JERZY'S WAR DIARY (cont.)

22nd January 1940
I report to the rallying station of the Polish Army in Paris.

7th February 1940
I work at the Polish Embassy in Paris in the postal section.

2nd & 3rd March 1940
Lille at Benia's.A

12th March 1940
Letters from Marysia, Theresa, Anula.B

19th April 1940
A card from Stach from Marseilles.

23rd April 1940
Temporary attachment to the Central Postal Office – 92, Rue de Varennes, Paris.

29th May 1940
18th Pomeranian Lancers Regimental Anniversary today.

10th June 1940
Departure from Paris – Versailles – Le Mans, By car.

11th June 1940
Angers – Chemille – staying 'till the 15th.

15th June 1940
Departure by train.

16th June 1940
Arriving in Saintes – staying 'till the 19th.

19th June 1940
Departure to the railway station – a night by the phone waiting for a call.

20th June 1940
Departure by car, Bordeaux – Le Verdon.

21st June 1940

In the woods now – waiting.

22nd June 1940

We embark the ships: 'Clan Fergusson' and 'Alderpool'.

24th June 1940

Arriving in Liverpool.

25th June 1940

We disembark – we are in England. We are to be transported by train to Glasgow – Scotland.

(continued...)

Many Polish servicemen arrived in Britain, particularly after the fall of France in late June 1940. By then, about 1,000 Polish naval personnel had previously evacuated to Scotland during the first months of the German attacks on Poland and a section of the Polish fleet had actually arrived there as early as 1 September 1939. A prior Agreement between Britain, Poland and France provided for Military and Naval cooperation between the three nations and on the first days of the invasion of Poland by Germany, in an effort to save some of its fleet, Poland sent the destroyers *BLYSKAWICA, GROM* and *BURZA* to Leith in Scotland.

By the end of 1939, approximately 2,000 Polish airmen had also been drafted into the Royal Air Force Volunteer Reserve and from the following year permission was given to form independent Polish groups, comprising fighter and bomber squadrons, balloon flight and Polish balloon barrage units – all acting under the operational command of the Royal Air Force.

As the German offensive made gains across northern Europe, there was a commonly held belief that the now unprotected eastern coastline of Scotland could become the target of an invasion or, at the very least, the focus of a diversionary assault by Germany from the direction of occupied Norway. During the fight for France, much of the Scottish 51st Highland Division (part of the II Corps of the British Expeditionary Force that had been sent to bolster French forces) was lost in battle. This heavy loss of Scottish-based servicemen would play a key part in the later decision to send the newly formed detachments of fleeing Polish soldiers in Britain, to initially assist in the defense of Scotland's eastern coast. Between 20,000 and 35,000 Polish soldiers began to arrive at various ports in England (Plymouth, Weymouth, Poole, Portsmouth, Southampton and Liverpool) and were transported by rail to Scotland to receive orders to assist in the construction, fortification and provision of the 24-hour patrol of the eastern Scottish coast (eventually between Montrose in the north, southwards to Burntisland – located on the north shore of the Firth of Forth). Duties would include the assembly of gun emplacements and anti-tank defenses, construction of concrete obstacles on beaches, building of observation posts and positioning fencing along stretches of coastline. The Poles were also able to assist the Royal Navy in the removal of mines that were frequently washed ashore.

The first weeks after arrival in Britain were reportedly difficult for the Poles. Many could not speak English; there was little or no news about the war in general and almost no information was available during the first few months about the situation in Poland itself. The soldiers were taken by rail from one location to the next, often having no real sense of where they were, a situation exacerbated by the frequent absence of signposts and railway station names that had been removed as a precaution and part of the overall war effort. The Poles' first impressions when arriving in England were nonetheless positive despite the chaos felt in the make-shift camps – where the food and sleeping arrangements were of a surprisingly high standard compared to what they had been used to. After the first few nights spent at open-air venues such as Haydock Park racecourse and the Ibrox stadium in Glasgow, when they were moved to other locations including camps at Lanark, Cupar, Tentsmuir, Crawford and Biggar, the Poles saw a return to field kitchens, open latrines and cold water in camps under canvas that had to be built by the Polish engineers themselves, many having little or no knowledge of British construction equipment and building methods that were in force at the time.

On *Jerzy's* arrival in Scotland on 25 June 1940, the formation of the military infrastructure required to support the Polish Army was taking shape. He recalls at first being marshalled with hundreds of other Polish soldiers inside what he believed to have been a 'dog stadium'. A short time later, *Jerzy* writes in his diary that he was moved to various temporary quarters in Carmichael.

As more premises were requisitioned throughout Scotland for use by the Polish Army for operations, support and administration, from 28 September 1940 the 1st Polish Corps began its formation and training with Gen. *Marian Kukiel* appointed as its commander on 3 October. Although the temporary Polish government and headquarters of the Polish General Staff were located in London, a sizeable portion of the Polish army and its command were situated in Scotland. The headquarters of the Polish Amy in Scotland at the time was at Eastend House, near Thankerton. Gradually, temporary barracks, Brigade headquarters, supply depots, Polish training schools, Polish hospitals, a Polish records office, a military staff college and a Polish recruitment bureau would be organized and a labyrinth of Polish bases would eventually cover large parts of Scotland. Polish soldiers dispersed throughout Scotland were accommodated in wooden barracks, Town Halls, YMCA buildings, boarding houses, hotels and private homes. During the early days of organization into units, some detachments of polish soldiers on Patrol in Scottish villages and towns were easily mistaken for French troops as they were still dressed in the French uniforms previously issued to them whilst previously in France.

The following list of towns and cities features in research undertaken by Robert Ostrycharz[6], into the deployment of Polish Forces during the Second World War in Scotland. Although by no means exhaustive, the list shows how widely spread throughout Scottish cities, towns and villages the detachments of Polish soldiers actually were: (© R M Ostrycharz):

	Dalkeith
Aberdeen	Douglas
Aberlady	Dunblane
Abernethy	Dundee
Alloa	Dunfermline
Alva	Dunkeld
Alyth	Duns
Angus	Duplin Castle nr. Perth
Arbroath	Earlsferry
Auchtermuchty	Earlston
Banchory, Kinkardineshire	Edinburgh
Biggar	Edleston
Blairgowrie	Elie – Fife
Brechin	Elts, Dundee
Bridge of Allan	Falkland
Bridge of Earn	Ferryden
Broughty Ferry	Fordoun, Kincardineshire
Buddon Camp, Angus	Forfar
Burrelton	Forres
Burntisland	Freuchie
Carmichael	Friockheim
Carnoustie	Galashiels
Cellardyke	Gilmerton nr. Crieff
Ceres, Fife	Gosford
Chirnside	Greenlaw
Clackmannan	Gullane
Coatbridge	Haddington
Coupar Angus	Hawick
Cowdenbeath	Inverarity
Crawford	Invergordon
Crieff	Inverurie, Aberdeenshire
Culter, Aberdeenshire	Irvine
Cupar	Johnstone
Dairsie	Kelso

Kelty	New Scone
Kenmore	Newburgh
Kincardine	Newport
Kinghorne	Newton
Kingskettle	Ormiston
Kinross	Penicuik
Kinrossie	Perth
Kirkcaldy	Polkemmet nr. Whitburn
Kirriemuir	Rattray
Ladybank	Rosemarkie
Lander	Rothsay
Largo	Selkirk
Letham	Springfield
Leuchars Airfield	St Andrews
Leven, Fife	Stenhousemuir
Linlithgow	Stonehaven
Longniddry	Stirling
Lossiemouth	Sunlaws
Marykirk	Taymouth Castle,
Meigle	Tayport, Westmuir
Melrose	Tentsmuir
Milnathort	Thankerton
Monkton, Ayrshire	Tillicoultry
Montrose	Walkerburn
Musselburgh	West Garleton

On 17 September 1940, *Jerzy* received confirmation of his appointment to the Polish Army's Headquarters Staff Unit at Eastend House, near Thankerton – where he remained as Adjutant for the following two years. This section was later relocated to Moncrief House, near Bridge of Earn, Perthshire in October 1940.

Having previously achieved near fluency in French, German and Russian, before long *Jerzy* started receiving formal lessons in English. On 1 September 1942, he was posted as Course Adjutant at the Polish Military Staff College at Kinghorn. The Staff College was transferred a few weeks later, to the Blackbarony Castle at Edleston near Peebles, on 21 September 1942. In addition to his duties at Edleston, Kinghorn and Peebles, his diary records the eighteen times between 1940 and 1944 that *Jerzy* travelled to London as a courier, carrying documents between the Polish military hub in Scotland and the offices of the Polish Government in Exile, (a body that would remain active in London until 1990; Britain however formally withdrew recognition of the Polish Government in Exile, on 6 July 1945).

30th June 1940

To Douglas.

10th July 1940

I go to Glasgow.

23rd July 1940

I depart for Douglas via Glasgow.

24th July 1940

I arrive in London, where I hand in the Central Postal Office files to the Polish Government in Exile.

1st August 1940

I leave London.

2nd August 1940

Carstairs, then Eastend - Thankerton, the Headquarters Command of the Polish Army in Scotland.
Broughton Camp.

4th August 1940

Edinburgh – Lt. Col. Alastair MacLean.

9th August 1940

I report my arrival and am assigned to the 1st Polish Corps Command Staff Headquarters at Eastend House, near Thankerton.

15th August 1940

I go to London as a courier for the first time.

16th August 1940

We move to the quarters in Carmichael.

24th August 1940

London – courier.

1st September 1940

I deliver a letter to the Commander-in-Chief in Kincardine – Col. Mitchel.
To Dunfermline, Earl of Elgin.
Minister Stroński at Queens Ferry, Edinburgh.

17th September 1940

I am appointed as the Officer in Charge of the Polish Army General Staff

Headquarters, Eastend House, Thankerton.

23rd September 1940
I travel to Rothesay via Glasgow.

26th September 1940
Major Eugeniusz Dąmbski reports. Major Kostkiewicz leaves.

27th to 29th September 1940
London with Stach.

30th September 1940
In the evening, I travel by car (a Simca) to Glasgow – Gen. Cory.

3rd October 1940
Major Kostkiewicz hands over and Major Dąmbski is appointed the Officer in Charge of the Polish 1st Corps Staff Headquarters.

5th October 1940
Equestrian competition in Edinburgh.

10th to 12th October 1940
To London as a courier.

16th October 1940
Funeral of Major Ruciński attached to the Armored Brigade based at Symington.

19th October 1940
The Polish 1st Corps Senior Staff are relocated to new quarters. I stay behind to shut-down the offices at Eastend House.

24th October 1940
I relocate to Moncrieff House, near Bridge of Earn, Perthshire.

25th to 27th October 1940
London as a courier.

3rd November 1940
St. Hubert's Day – a walk in the mountains.

19th November 1940
I send four telegrams via Lt. Czajkowski.

25th to 27th November 1940
London as a courier.

29th November 1940

Departure of Col. Liebich to London – Col. Krubski.

30th November 1940

It has been 15 months since the outbreak of the war.

1st December 1940

Reception at Miss Crabbie's – Butterstone House.

3rd December 1940

I visit Stach in Arbroath.

5th to 7th December 1940

London as a courier.

10th December 1940

Light Cavalry Regiment Festival – Perth. Ball in Kincardine at Col. Mitchel's.

17th December 1940

Reception at Lord Provost's in Perth.

24th December 1940

Christmas Eve, Mr. President, Gen. Sikorski.

27th to 29th December 1940

London as a courier.

1941

14th to 21st January 1941

Holiday leave – Cranmer Hall – Tel. Fakenham 114 – Norfolk – the Jones's.

21st to 25th January 1941

War game.

26th January 1941

Reception for the Scots in Perth – Station Hotel.

28th January 1941

Forfar, Arbroath, Stach, Dundee.

31st January 1941

Telegram from Nice from Ms. Niekraszewicz.

4th February 1941

Telegram from Fryburg from Ms. Studzińska.

10th to 13th February 1941

London as a courier.

20th February 1941

Edinburgh as a courier.

22nd February 1941

Arrival of Col. Liebich. – Stach in the evening.

22nd to 25th February 1941

London as a courier.

25th February 1941

Second Lt. Jan Herse leaves for London, then, as a translator with Col. Liebich, to Ankara.

1st March 1941

Telephone conversation with Tadeusz Grabowski in London. Today it has been a year and a half since the start of the war. In the evening, we watch the Northern Lights.

5th March 1941

Dundee with Lt. Tabian – Albany Terrace 10.

7th March 1941

Forfar – King, Queen – parade.

Polish troops being evacuated from France to England, 24 June 1940

9th March 1941
Gen. Sikorski and the National Council members.

12th March 1941
Dupplin Castle – X-ray.

15th March 1941
Glasgow was bombed in the night.

(continued...)

Polish troops being evacuated from France to England, 24 June 1940

EXTRACT FROM JERZY'S WAR DIARY (cont.)

16th March 1941
Reception at Miss Crabbie's.

18th March 1941
Capt. Kozubowski departs.

22nd March 1941
Gathering of cavalry officers in Arbroath.

23rd March 1941
Arbroath – Stach.

25th March 1941
Letter from Mr. Gustaw Zieliński dated 14.12.1940.

1st April 1941
Major Minkiewicz is transferred to London to Gen. Głuchowski's.

6th April 1941
Germany attacks Yugoslavia.

8th April 1941
Lady Fay Ansruther (née Recknitz) takes my suitcase to Carmichael House, Thankerton, Lanarkshire.

13th April 1941
Easter.

13th to 14th April 1941
Stach and I go via Glasgow to Rothesay and Tighnabruaich.

17th April 1941
I go to London as a courier.

23rd April 1941
News of J. Herse's death in Egypt.

29th April 1941
Second Lt. Adam Daszewski departs – transferred.

3rd May 1941
Clocks move 24 hours. (actually just one hour)

5th to 6th May 1941
Alarm in the night – bombing of Glasgow.

11th May 1941
Gen. Sosnkowski injured by a bomb in London.

13th May 1941
Rudolf Hess has flown over from Germany to Scotland.

18th May 1941
Butterstone.

29th May 1941
Festival of the 18th Uhlans Regiment – Forfar with Gen. Dembiński. Taymouth Castle.

4th June 1941
General Haller arrives.

5th June 1941
I receive two letters: from Ms. Studzińska and Ms. Niekraszewicz.

6th June 1941
Lt. Janusz Kruszyński departs to London.

8th June 1941
Gathering of the former soldiers of the Polish Armed Forces in the East – in Perth.

10th June 1941
I receive a letter from Ms. Porret C

11th June 1941
Lt. Czajkowski departs to London.

13th June 1941
Arbroath at Stach's.

22nd June 1941
Germany attacks Russia.

(continued...)

Polish soldiers beside ordnance on the beach at Arbroath, Scotland 1941

Engineers of the 1st Rifle Brigade (1st Polish Corps) constructing beach defenses at Tentsmuir, 11 November 1940. The concrete blocks were used as anti-tank obstacles.

From the Imperial War Museum Collection of images of THE POLISH ARMY IN BRITAIN, 1940-1947 Image supplied under license © Imperial War Museum (H 5493) LIC-15996-V8Q5B9

EXTRACT FROM JERZY'S WAR DIARY (cont.)

23rd to 26th June 1941
London, as a courier.

30th June 1941
J. I. Paderewski dies.

5th July 1941
Farewell to Major Fieldorf in Perth.

7th to 9th July 1941
London, as a courier.

13th July 1941
Dunkeld and Butterstone with Stach.

20th July 1941
Concert at Dunkeld Cathedral.

21st July 1941
10th Armored Brigade comes to Scone.

25th July 1941
Taymouth Castle – Hospital No. 1 – with Lt. Col. Kycia.

27th July 1941
Perth, Crieff, Comrie, St. Fillans with Stach and Tadeusz Jaroński.

29th July 1941
News of signing an agreement with Russia.

1st August 1941
Gen. Szyszko-Bohusz goes to Russia.

5th August 1941
First lesson with Mrs. Crichton at Bridge of Earn.

8th to 9th August 1941
Exercise "Rabbit"

10th August 1941
Clocks go back 24 hours.

10th to 12th August 1941
London, as a courier.

17th to 19th August 1941
Course in Tentsmuir.

29th August 1941
Capt. Loga departs to London and Russia.

2nd September 1941
Lecture by Gen. Januszajtis.
Cavalry Capt. Hławaty and 274 officers depart to Africa.

8th September 1941
I send a letter to Borys Zalewski in Stockholm.

11th _September 1941_

Farewell to Lt. Col. Ogórkiewicz from the 3rd Division to the 1st Brigade.

12th _September 1941_

Arrival of counsel Retinger – Bereswell Club in Perth.

13th _September 1941_

Farewell to Cavalry Cap. Hlawaty.

14th _September 1941_

Dundee with Stach.

20th _September 1941_

Prime Minister Churchill visits our troops.

22nd _September 1941_

Major Dąmbski's car accident.

23rd _September 1941_

Shows in the Parachute Brigade.

25th _September 1941_

Gen. Sikorski – decoration.

27th _September 1941_

Farewell to Gen. Zając.

28th _September 1941_

Scone at the 10th Regiment of Mounted Riflemen.

8th _October 1941_

Poland – Czechoslovakia football match in Perth.

9th _October 1941_

London as a courier

24th _October 1941_

Funeral of Minister Lieberman in London.

28th _October 1941_

Funeral of Cavalry Capt. Jerzy Baliński in Perth.

30th _October 1941_

London as a courier.

9th _November 1941_

Departure of Major Wojtczak.

<u>10th November 1941</u>

Lecture by Prof. Komarnicki and prof. Grabski at the 11th Signal Company.

<u>13th November 1941</u>

Lecture by ex-MP Mastek.

<u>15th November 1941</u>

Lecture by Prof. Grabski.

<u>20th November 1941</u>

Capt. Wiktor Brummer dies.

<u>21st November 1941</u>

Holiday leave with Stach in London. Windsor – Eton.

<u>1st to 6th December 1941</u>

Lectures by ex-MP M. Mastek, whom I drive around the Corps.

<u>10th December 1941</u>

Holy Mass in Dundee – Anniversary of the 1st Light Cavalry Regiment Festival.

<u>24th December 1941</u>

Christmas Eve.

(continued...)

Their Majesties *King George VI* and *Queen Elizabeth* visiting Polish Troops in Arbroath, Scotland 1941

Jerzy Dobiecki, Scotland 1941
(This photograph was carried by *Jerzy's* brother, *Stanisław*, for the duration of the war)

EXTRACT FROM JERZY'S WAR DIARY (cont.)

1942

1st January 1942
Moncrieff House – Bridge of Earn – Perthshire.

2nd to 4th January 1942
London, as a courier.

8th to 11th January 1942
London, as a courier.

12th January 1942
I take on the adjutant duties to cover for the ill Cavalry Capt. Glazer until 12.3.

24th January 1942
Gen. Thorn and Gen. Cory decorate Lt. Col. Deskur and Major Baltusis with British awards.

17th January 1942
General Kukiel receives the Order of the Bath, 3rd class.

18th to 19th February 1942
Exercise in Stirling.

5th March 1942
Reserve Lieutenant Sielski is assigned.

12th March to 2nd April 1942
English course in Edinburgh. I return to Moncrieff House.

10th April 1942
I go to Falkirk to assist the arrival of the Corps.

13th April 1942
I get otitis media – I go to the Paderewski Hospital in Edinburgh.

(continued...)

(left to right)
General *Stanisław Maczek* (Officer commanding Polish 1st Armored Division)
General *Kazimierz Sosnkowski* (from 1943, Commander-in-Chief of Polish forces) and,
General *Marian Kukiel* (General Officer Commanding Polish 1st Corps)

Arbroath, Scotland 4 July 1941

7th May 1942
I return to Falkirk.

11th May 1942
Lt. Janusz Kruszyński transferred to Edinburgh.

12th May 1942
I drive Rev. Zdzisław Obertyński to 16th Tank Brigade in Duns.

14th May 1942
I go to live at the Hopkinses' – Reres, High Station Road, Falkirk.

28th May to 1st June 1942
Holiday leave in London.

6th June 1942
Gen. Burchard Bukacki dies.

16th June 1942
Major January Suchodolski, Gen. Kossakowski and others depart to the Middle East.

18th June 1942
I receive two cards from JaniaD dated 18.5.1942.

24th June 1942
I report to Col. Zakrzewski in the Training Brigade.

26th June to 31st August 1942
Auchtertool – Sorting Camp. Major Słatyński.
From 30.6. – Major Łoziński.

26th August 1942
Duke of Kent dies.

(continued...)

(Left to Right)
General *Stanisław Maczek* (Officer commanding 1st Polish Armored Division)
General *Stanisław Kopański* (3rd Carpathian Rifle Division)
Lieutenant General *Władysław Anders* (prior to his appointment as commander of the Polish 2nd Corps)
Galashiels, Scotland 25 April 1942

EXTRACT FROM JERZY'S WAR DIARY (cont.)

1st September 1942
Assignment to the Military Staff College as Course Adjutant – Kinghorn.

3rd to 7th September 1942
Holiday leave with Stach – Penzance. St. Ives – Cornwall. London.

15th September 1942
Lt. Col. Rozner dies.

21st September 1942
We transfer to Eddleston near Peebles – Black Barony Hotel.
I go to live at Miss Turnbull's, 103 North Gate, Rowanbrae, Peebles.

28th September 1942
The 2nd Course of the Military Staff College starts.

21st October 1942
Gen. Boruta-Spiechowicz, Gen. Cory, Col. de Chaire and others visit the School.

28th October 1942
Czechoslovakian Festival.

11th November 1942
Anniversary of the Uprising. Reception for the Scots.

14th December 1942
Birthday of King George VI (1895).

18th December 1942
Cavalry Captain Zabielski.

19th to 23rd December 1942
Holiday leave with Stach in Falkirk at the Hopkinses'.

24th December 1942
Christmas Eve.

(continued...)

General *Władysław Sikorski*, Commander-in-Chief of the Polish Forces in Exile, on Inspection, Britain 1942

General *Władysław Sikorski*, Commander-in-Chief of the Polish Forces in Exile, on Inspection, Britain 1942

Barony Castle (formerly Blackbarony Castle), Edleston near Peebles, Scotland used during WWII as the Polish Military Staff College
(Image © De Vere Hotels)

Jerzy's diary mentions the numerous occasions that he was able to meet up with his brother, *Stanisław* ('*Stach*'), who was also then stationed in Scotland. As a Lieutenant with the Polish 24th Lancers Regiment, the unit was also part of the 1st Polish Corps (and later the 1st Polish Armored Division – formed officially in February 1942, under the command of Gen. *Stanisław Maczek*).

Jerzy and his brother *Stach* were very close, visiting one another whenever they could. *Jerzy* records their meetings in London, Peebles, Galashiels, Arbroath, Edinburgh, Dundee and other venues throughout England. They wrote to each other frequently and *Stanisław* would even write to *Jerzy* in Scotland from the fighting in Normandy, later in 1944. As an indication of the degree of administrative organization that had been put in place to support the Polish Army in Britain, amongst some of *Jerzy's* correspondence there are letters bearing Polish-issue stamps – Polish stamps of varying denomination of the Polish *Złoty*, that had actually been printed in Edinburgh. In order to enable improved communication between Polish servicemen attached to the Polish Army throughout Britain and so as to generate revenue for the Polish Cause, in agreement with the British authorities a limited Polish Postal Service was introduced in December 1941 by Poland's Government in Exile. The issue and use of Polish stamps had the added value of advertising to the world, Poland's armed forces' continuing struggle. Letters bearing these 'foreign' stamps were passed through and handled as normal UK-bound mail.

On 13 December 1943, *Jerzy* was posted to the Polish Infantry training Centre at Burntisland, where he remained until the Spring of the following year.

Following training and maneuvers in May 1943, the operational units of the Polish 1st Armored Division were mobilized in March 1944 and relocated to Tilbury Docks in the south of England. The Division remained here on stand-by for the eventual transfer with the rest of the Allied Forces across the Channel to Normandy, in what has become known as the 'D' Day Landings. The allies started landing on the French coast during the morning of 6 June 1944 and the operation to transfer troops, equipment and supplies across the Channel would actually last for several months. Following a few days' preparation for transport by ship, elements of the Polish Armored Division arrived in France, at *Courseuilles-sur-Mer*, on the Normandy coast (designated 'Juno' beach) between 30 July and 4 August (D-Day + 54). The 1st Polish Armored Division assembled near *Bayeux*, initially as part of the Canadian 1st Corps but later was attached to the 2nd Canadian Corps – commanded by Lt. Gen. *Guy Simonds*, prior to deployment in the battles south of *Caen*, (notably near *Falaise* and *Mont Ormel*).

The 1st Polish Independent Parachute Brigade commanded by Maj. Gen. *Stanisław Sosabowski*, would have to wait until September 1944 before it would be sent into the theatre of operations on the continent. The Brigade was flown from England in support of the British 1st Airborne Division, in Operation 'Market Garden'.

Jerzy remained on administrative duty in Scotland whilst the operational units of the Polish army fought their way through Northern Europe as part of the Allied Forces' drive to liberate France, Belgium and Holland. When the Polish 1st Armored Division eventually arrived in Germany, it was deployed in the fighting as far as Berlin and the Division was given the task of accepting the surrender of German forces at the port of Wilhelmshaven.

On 7 December 1944, *Jerzy* himself made his way from Southampton to Le Havre in France and then to Paris, prior to eventually re-joining, as a liaison officer, the command of the Polish 1st Armored Division in its occupation duties in the Western Allied Occupation Zone of Germany. He remained on the continent until September 1945.

Correspondence bearing Polish stamps and posted in Britain in 1942 received by Capt. *Jerzy Dobiecki* and his brother *Stanisław* whilst attached to the 1st Polish Corps

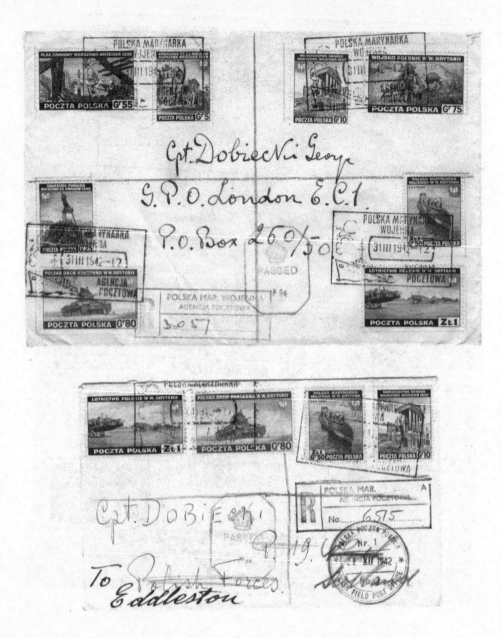

Correspondence bearing Polish stamps and posted in Britain in 1942 received by Capt. *Jerzy Dobiecki* whilst attached to the Polish 1st Polish Corps

(left to right)
Brother '*Stach*' (*Stanisław Dobiecki*) and *Jerzy*
Scotland c1943

EXTRACT FROM JERZY'S WAR DIARY (cont.)

1943

1ˢᵗ *January 1943*
Peebles – snow.

13ᵗʰ *January 1943*
Visiting the Navy, "Duke of York" and others.

17ᵗʰ *January 1943*
Falkirk – As Chairman.

7ᵗʰ *January 1943*
Stach at mine.

10ᵗʰ *January 1943*
Col. Liebich – lecture on Turkey.

21ˢᵗ *January 1943*
Stach at mine.

22nd to 24th January 1943
Falkirk, As Chairman.

9th March 1943
Galashiels at Stach's.

25th March 1943
Air raid siren – bombs near Eddleston.

31st March 1943
End of the 2nd Course at the Military Staff College.

3rd to 5th April 1943
Falkirk, Chairman.

6th April 1943
Snow and frost.

9th April 1943
With Stach – Glasgow.

13th April 1943
Col. Smoleński hands the Military Staff College over to Col. Korewo.

25th April 1943
I go to Stach's to Galashiels.

4th May 1943
After dinner, at the park in the sunshine – a nap.

8th May 1943
At Stach's in Galashiels – rain.

9th to 10th May 1943
Snow.

13th May 1943
Stach becomes a Corporal.

17th to 19th May 1943
In London.

24th to 29th May 1943
"A Week of Studies".

30th to 31st May 1943
London, 29th Anniversary of the Festival of the 18. Uhlans Regiment.

2ⁿᵈ June 1943
Stach at mine.

6ᵗʰ June 1943
At Stach's in Galashiels.

13ᵗʰ June 1943
Falkirk – As Chairman – overnight stay.

17ᵗʰ June 1943
Departure of Lieut. Słowakiewicz.

19ᵗʰ June 1943
Departure of Major Dziewiszek to hospital.

28ᵗʰ June 1943
Opening of the Air Force College.

29ᵗʰ June 1943
All day in the sunshine.

30ᵗʰ June 1943
To Falkirk – in a Humber – I bathe in the river Tweed.

4ᵗʰ July 1943
Dawyck – at Mr and Mrs Balfour's (she is a sister of Montagu Norman).

4ᵗʰ July 1943
Accident of Gen. Sikorski in Gibraltar.

10ᵗʰ July 1943
News of the invasion of Sicily.

12ᵗʰ July 1943
Start of the 3ʳᵈ Command Course at the Military Staff College.

(continued...)

Polish soldiers in Galashiels, Scotland 1943

Polish soldiers in a queue outside the cinema
Galashiels, Scotland 1943

EXTRACT FROM JERZY'S WAR DIARY (cont.)

17th and 18th July 1943
In the sun – golf course.

24th and 25th July 1943
In the sun – golf course.

26th July 1943
Mussolini resigns.

30th July 1943
Col. Mac. Iżycki arrives.

3rd August 1943
At the Military Staff College, Gen. Zając, Col. Krubski, Lieut. Col. Rudnicki, Lieut. Rostworowski.

4th August 1943
Birthday of Queen Elizabeth (born on 4/8/1900 as Lady E. Bowes Lyon, daughter of Earl of Strathmore).

17th August 1943
Hunting in Dawyck at Mr and Mrs Balfour's.

24th August 1943
Falkirk Corps – Col. Smoliński.

27th to 30th August 1943
London at S. H. – Stach.

1st September 1943
4 years since the war started.

7th September 1943
Józio Żółtowski departs to the air force.

8th September 1943
Gen. and Mrs Dembiński in Peebles.

19th September 1943
Stach's birthday ('05).

25th September 1943
2 cards – parcel receipt confirmations.

3rd October 1943
Stach at mine.

9th October 1943
Falkirk, As Chairman.

13th October 1943
Italy declares war on Germany.

31st October 1943
Stach at mine.

24th November 1943
Edinburgh & Falkirk.

27th November 1943
Edinburgh, at Tadeusz Łoś's

30th November 1943
Churchill's birthday (69).

1st December 1943
Edinburgh – Tadeusz Łoś.

(continued...)

MINISTERSTWO
INFORMACJI I DOKUMENTACJI
Placowka w Szkocji

POLISH MINISTRY OF INFORMATION
Scottish Office
DMT/2032

43 Charlotte Square
Edinburgh
Tel.: 32909   Telegr.: POLMOI
15th November, 194 3

Dear Sir,

We have been in touch with Blackbarony, and have been assured
that it will be quite all right for you and Mr. Cameron to go
there on Friday, 19th November at about 3:30 p.m. You should
ask to see either Mr. Robinson, the owner, who lives in the
house, or Capt. Dobiecki, who is in charge.

Lt. Col. The Hon. Arthur Murray,
C.M.G., D.S.O.,
23 Waterloo Place,
Edinburgh.

Yours faithfully,

(Jan K. Roehr)

Sample of correspondence crossing the desk of Captain Jerzy Dobiecki, whilst posted
as Adjutant at the Polish Military Staff College, temporarily located at Barony Castle
Scotland 1943

EXTRACT FROM JERZY'S WAR DIARY (cont.)

3rd December 1943
To Edinburgh (in a Hillman).

6th December 1943
Lieut. Col. Grabowski arrives at the Military Staff College.

13th December 1943
Order – I am posted to the Infantry Training Centre.

14th December 1943
Birthday of King George VI (1895).

16th December 1943
Arrival of Lieut. Gebethner.

17th December 1943
I drive Gen. Kopański from Edinburgh.

18th December 1943
End of the 3rd Command Course at the Military Staff College.

21st December 1943
Edinburgh – Stach.

24th December 1943
Christmas Eve at H. L.

29th December 1943
I drive Ms. Chodacka to Edinburgh.

31st December 1943
Last day as adjutant at the Military Staff College.

(Continued...)

(left to right) *Jerzy's* daughters *Anna ("Anita")* and *Theresa*
Poland 1943

Prime Minister *Winston Churchill* on the steps of the Brompton Oratory, Kensington,
following a church service with Polish soldiers,
London 1943

Stanisław Dobiecki (Jerzy's brother) (right of picture) and colleague, 24th Polish Lancers, 1st Polish Armored Division on exercise, somewhere in England c1943

Stanisław Dobiecki (2nd from left) with colleagues of 24th Polish Lancers, 1st Polish Armored Division, Scotland c1943

Gen. *Stanisław Maczek* – Commander Polish 1st Armored Division and
Gen. *Bernard Montgomery* – Commander-in-Chief British 8th Army (shaking hands)
meeting Polish Officers of the 1st Polish Armored Division, England 1943

Left to right (front rank):
Col. *T. Majewski* – Officer Commanding 10th Polish Cavalry Brigade
Maj. *S. Koszutski* – Officer Commanding 2nd Polish Armored Regiment
Col. *W. Zgorzelski* – Officer Commanding 10th Polish Dragoon Regiment
Maj. *J. W. Kański* – Officer Commanding 24th Polish Lancers Regiment
Left to right (rear rank):
Maj. *A. Stefanowicz* – Officer Commanding 1st Armored Regiment.
Cavalry Capt. M. Czarnecki.

EXTRACT FROM JERZY'S WAR DIARY (cont.)

1944

1st January 1944
Peebles.

3rd January 1944
Falkirk as Chairman.

10th January 1944
I pass the adjutant duties at the Military Staff College to Lieut. Wacław Gebethner.

15th January 1944
Falkirk as Chairman.

16th January 1944
Lanark with Ms. Mar. Demb'.

27th to 30th January 1944
London.

1st February 1944
I report my departure and say my goodbyes in Peebles.

2nd February 1944
I go to Burntisland.

4th February 1944
Military Management Course.

19th to 21st February 1944
Stach at mine (20th – to Edinburgh, Lieut. Pietrzyski).

26th March 1944
I meet Stach in Edinburgh.

5th April 1944
End of the Management Course.

6th to 18th April 1944
Easter Holidays.

8th to 10th April 1944
Falkirk as Chairman.

12th to 18th April 1944
Balholmie – Mr and Mrs Moon – Meikleour.

19th April 1944
Lauder at Stach's.

21st April 1944
(1926) – Birthday of Princess Elizabeth.

1st May 1944
To Edinburgh, headquarters of the Military Units in Great Britain.

3rd May 1944
Edinburgh, Stach.

8th May 1944
A phone-call to Stach – his Names-day.

9th May 1944
Stirling.

11th to 14th May 1944
London as a courier.

20th May 1944
Falkirk, as Chairman.

19th to 31st May 1944
12 days of leave.

27th May 1944
I leave for London.

29th May 1944
Holy Mass (Requiem Mass) – Festival of the 18. Ułan Regiment.

3rd to 15th June 1944
Course at the Department of Social Security in London (re Repatriation).

18th June 1944
In the evening, I leave London.

19th June 1944
I arrive, via Burntisland, at Dunfermline.

24ᵗʰ June 1944
Edinburgh – Falkirk as Chairman.

27ᵗʰ June 1944
2 parcel receipt confirmations from Mar. and Anula from January 1944.

5ᵗʰ July 1944
Stach sends £10.

10ᵗʰ to 12ᵗʰ July 1944
I move suitcases from Falkirk to Edinburgh – Red Cross, 15 Rutland Street.

10ᵗʰ August 1944
Letter from Stach from Normandy.

(continued...)

March-past of Polish troops (Engineers)
Arbroath, Scotland 1944

U.S. Gen. *Dwight Eisenhower*, Supreme Allied Commander, with
Gen. *Stanisław Maczek*, Commander-in-chief 1st Polish Armored Division,
France 1944

EXTRACT FROM JERZY'S WAR DIARY (cont.)

1ˢᵗ September 1944
5 years since the war started.

3ʳᵈ September 1944
Anniversary of the declaration of war by Britain.

17ᵗʰ September 1944
Jagielski and others – moved to London.

23rd September 1944
Together with others, I also receive an order to move to London.

25ᵗʰ September 1944
We leave Dunfermline.

26ᵗʰ September 1944
We arrive in London.

4ᵗʰ October 1944
Jurek and others fly to Paris.

12ᵗʰ October 1944
At Gen. and Mrs Dembiński's.

7ᵗʰ December 1944
Departure from London to Southampton.

8ᵗʰ December 1944
Arrival at Le Havre.

12ᵗʰ December 1944
Arrival in Paris.

20ᵗʰ December 1944
Lille – at Benia's.

23ʳᵈ December 1944
Departure from Paris to Romilly, "Les Champs" near Maizières.

- End of Jerzy's Diaries -

Notes to *Jerzy's* diary

A '*Benia*' was the family's nick-name given to *Jerzy's* sister-in-law - *Gabriela* (wife *Maria's* sister)

B '*Marysia*' diminutive in polish for *Maria*. '*Anula*' diminutive in Polish for *Anna* (wife Maria's sister)

C Ms *Porret* - Brother *Kazimierz's* wife

D '*Jania*' - *Jerzy's* sister

On the night of the 12 and 13 February 1944, *Kazimierz Dobiecki* – *Jerzy's* younger brother, whilst at home in Poland at his estate of *Terebiniec* (about 31km north-west of **Poturzyn)** together with his wife Odette and six other villagers, were murdered by a group of partisans. This area of rural eastern Poland at this time was in a state of great confusion and had fallen into virtual anarchy. Since the preceding month, when Russian forces had once again crossed the border into Poland, what remained of German military units were harried by partisan groups of different origins. Additionally, local people forced from their homes together with small bands of army deserters, Ukrainian and other criminal groups or gangs roamed the forests and the countryside, living off the land and regularly robbed and looted local isolated villages, settlements, farms and remote manor houses.

Kazimierz and *Odette* were subsequently laid to rest at the cemetery at **Hrubieszów**.

Six months later, in August of 1944, Jerzy lost his sister-in-law, *Zofia* (*Maria's* sister), who had been recruited into the Polish Home Army and was killed during the **Warsaw** Uprising.

Kazimierz Dobiecki
Poland c1938

Odette Dobiecka (née de Porret)
wife of *Kazimierz*, Poland c1940

Zofia Breza (Jerzy's sister-in-law)
Poland c1940

CHAPTER 9
POLISH RESETTLEMENT CORPS
England (1946-1948)

Following Germany's surrender in May 1945 and with the war coming to an end, *Jerzy* returned to England in September 1945. At the time of his arrival in London, news and rumor of the developing and worsening situation under communist rule in Poland started to reach the Polish soldiers who like Jerzy, were returning to England with no idea of what their future might now hold. As well as Jerzy's immediate concern for his family in Poland, his own position and prospects as an officer in the Polish army, were very unclear.

Although the actual fighting of the war was over, one of *Jerzy's* first thoughts was for *Maria* – his wife, and for the welfare of the three children. *Jerzy* had not actually heard whether they were safe or where or under what conditions they were currently living in Poland; although he had received some correspondence from *Maria* during his posting in Scotland, he could not be certain that he had a home left to go to. Between November 1942 and 1943, in south eastern Poland where the family had been living, the German authorities had removed Polish families from hundreds of villages in the vicinity of **Zamość,** in an attempt to make the area suitable for eventual German settlement. The family homes at **Radostów** and **Poturzyn** were only fifty kilometers away and it was quite conceivable that these neighborhoods had also been caught up in the net.

The situation in Poland immediately following the end of the war, was really quite bleak. Much of the country lay in ruins, its infrastructure and essential services were in chaos; no effective state authority was yet firmly in control and poverty, homelessness, famine and disease were widespread. The personal loss, destitution and destruction caused havoc for the daily lives of millions who were now having to survive in desperate conditions in what remained of Poland's villages, towns and cities. The human cost of the war on Poland was unimaginable; a million orphans were left after the killing of six million civilians. 500,000 men and women were lost in battle and many thousands were now invalid.

In 1945, although several million displaced Poles began to return to Poland, almost as many were on the move and fleeing the now advancing Red Army. In the wake of the Agreements previously reached at Yalta (Soviet Union) in February 1945 and subsequently at *Potsdam* (Germany) in July that year, huge population transfers occurred between Poland, Czechoslovakia, Hungary and Germany. As Poland fell under Soviet control, it lost large sections of its territory in the west and was being forced to incorporate others in the east. Poland was not alone in the process – that was being implemented across parts of eastern Europe in an effort to convert countries into communist states. To varying degrees, independence was now being stripped from the Soviet-occupied countries of the Peoples' Republic of Hungary, Peoples' Republic of Romania, Peoples' Republic of Albania and, eventually, the German Democratic Republic (East Germany). In Poland, fresh from five years of German occupation, the country was quite quickly subjected to another reign of terror, and repression would once again be dealt-out to its people. In the two years that followed the end of the war, thousands of Poles would lose their lives as about 80,000[1] continued to fight with units of Poland's former underground Army and other guerilla groups against Polish and Russian state secret Police.

To many, Russia was still regarded as a British and American ally. It was inconceivable to the Poles living in the west that Poland could again be subjected to a further period of barbarity as that just experienced under the years of German occupation. In truth, state censorship over reporting ensured the news was not widely reported outside Poland. Through a campaign of terror, authoritarianism and subtle administrative persecution, anti-communists and those considered to be 'enemies of the state' in Poland were steadily removed from positions of importance in every field of authority and influence. Military tribunals prosecuted those incriminated of crimes against the state and harsh sentences were routinely handed-out for minor infringements of the law. Polish citizens, secretly reported to the authorities by an ever-increasing network of informants, were routinely investigated by state agencies – often on the basis of spurious hearsay evidence. Huge numbers of Poles would be rounded-up and deported to the Soviet Union during the years that followed. Many hundreds of rural estates, areas of arable land, large farms and properties such as those owned by *Jerzy* and his family at **Radostów** and **Poturzyn**, were seized by the government and redistributed by the state authorities without any compensation given to their owners. Property formerly belonging to German families was nationalized and the families forcibly resettled or eliminated. Territories in the east that were about to be transferred under the post-war Peace Agreement, had much of their factory-resources and equipment sent to the Soviet Union from where the communist regime began transformation of post-war Poland into a Soviet satellite state. Polish soldiers in Britain started to receive letters from their families in Poland in which some of the hardships were alluded-to, either in coded format or through the use of a careful choice of words. The fear of retribution from the authorities in Poland was such that some Poles even wrote from Poland to relatives in England under an alias.

There was some independent foreign reporting of the developing situation in Poland, and accounts that were able to filter through Polish state censorship began also to reach the government in London. Here, there was already a degree of anxiety over some of the major domestic social issues of the day. General uncertainty about what would happen now that the war was over, was perhaps reflected in the outcome of the general election, held on 5 July 1945 in the UK. In a surprise result, Winston Churchill and the Conservative Party were replaced by Clement Atlee's Labor Party. Amongst the immediate concerns before the new parliament, were the acute national shortage of housing and a need for urgent post-war economic development. The pressing concern over what to do with the huge numbers of Polish soldiers, who would now have to be demobilized, temporarily housed and possibly reskilled, merely compounded the problem.

During the war about 249,000 Polish soldiers had been enlisted into units that had been deployed under British command. The Provisional Government established in Poland following the end of the war, suggested that the Polish soldiers returning to Britain after the end of hostilities on the continent, should be repatriated to Poland and placed under the control of officers appointed by the authorities in Warsaw. The British Foreign Office initially had some reservations about this proposal and found itself having to appease a Polish Government that had set-itself up in exile in London (and which it did not officially recognize), whilst simultaneously dealing with a Polish People's 'puppet' communist-led provisional government established in Poland – which it did recognize.

The question on *Jerzy*'s lips and on those of the thousands of Poles like him was whether they should now return to Poland on moral grounds and assist in the re-building of their nation, despite Poland's slow descent into communism. Many had painful memories of what it was like to live under Russian-rule before the war and returning home represented a replay of a previous existence under a regime that would now not baulk at punishing them for having sided with the forces of the West.

In 1945, it was not immediately clear how many Poles sought a return to Poland from Britain or how great a number wished to seek exile in Britain or her territories. Anti-alien sentiment was already running high and British workers were showing signs of fear for their own jobs. Of the 10,000 or so most highly qualified within all ranks of the Polish army offering skills such as those associated with professorship of universities, doctors, chemists, members of the judiciary, teachers and engineers, large numbers were unable to speak English sufficiently well to be able to carry on their professions in Britain. Equally, many simply did not possess the necessary skills that were urgently required for the immediate post-war economic effort in Britain. Those similar in age to *Jerzy* were in a bracket where re-training and assimilation into industry would become a very tough challenge for all concerned.

The following year the British government appealed to the members of the Polish forces directly. On 20 /21 March 1946, in what was to become known as operation 'KEYNOTE' it distributed a leaflet to every serving Polish soldier in Britain, signed by Foreign Secretary Earnest Bevin, informing the Poles that the government in Warsaw saw it as the duty of the Polish soldiers, seamen and airmen to go back and to help to re-build Poland and to assist with the country's return to prosperity. An assurance was given that in exchange, the Polish servicemen would receive full military honors in line with those accorded them whilst engaged with the British army. The Appeal to members of the Polish Forces read as follows[2]:

MESSAGE FROM THE BRITISH FOREIGN SECRETARY TO ALL MEMBERS OF THE POLISH FORCES UNDER BRITISH COMMAND.

His Majesty's Government have many times made it clear that it is their policy to assist the greatest possible number of members of the Polish Armed Forces under British Command to return to Poland of their own free will and in conditions worthy of their great services to the Allied cause. In accordance with this policy they have in recent months been in negotiation with the Polish Provisional Government of National Unity, which the British Government, like other Governments, regard as the only authority entitled to speak on behalf of Poland, regarding the conditions upon which returning Polish soldiers, sailors and air men will be received back in their own country. As a result of these negotiations the Provisional Government has furnished His Majesty's Government with a statement setting forth its policy on this question. The text of this statement is annexed.

The British Government regard this statement as satisfactory. In the light of these assurances they have reviewed the position of the Polish Armed Forces under British Command. They consider it to be the duty of all members of those Forces who possibly can do so to return to their home country without further delay under the conditions now offered them in order that they may make their contribution to the restoration of the prosperity of liberated Poland. Only thus can they serve their country in a manner worthy of her great traditions.

Those who nevertheless feel compelled to remain abroad in full knowledge of the present situation will be treated as far as our resources permit with due recognition of their gallant service. In execution of the policy announced by Mr. Winston Churchill, the British Government will give, in collaboration with other Governments, such assistance as is in their power to enable those who fought with us throughout the war to start a new life outside Poland with their families and dependents. But the British Government, after the most careful examination of the whole problem, are bound to make it plain that they can promise no more than this. There is no question of the Polish Army, Navy or Air Forces at present under British Command being preserved by the British Government as in dependent armed forces abroad, and it is the intention of the British Government to disband as soon as practicable those men who decide not to return to Poland. Nor can the British Government offer to the members of the Polish Armed Forces under British command any guarantee that they will all be enabled to settle in British territory at home or overseas.

I appeal on behalf of the British Government to every individual member of the Polish Armed Forces to consider carefully the alternatives which are here set before him. I earnestly trust that the overwhelming majority will decide to avail themselves of this opportunity, especially as I am not in a position to guarantee that there will be a further opportunity for them to return to Poland.

Speaking on behalf of the British Government, I declare that it is in the best interests of Poland that you should return to her now, when she requires the help of all her sons in the arduous task of reconstructing the country and making good the devastation caused by the war.

ERNEST BEVIN.
(©Parliamentary information, licensed under the Open Parliament License v3.0. https://www.parliament.uk/site-information/copyright-parliament/open-parliament-licence/)

The measure did little to inspire many Polish service personnel who in some cases, refused to take a leaflet when it was officially presented to them by their senior officers. General Anders openly urged those he commanded not to return to Poland. Pressure and ostracism by their comrades were applied to those who voiced notions of voluntarily returning to Poland. The most patriotic amongst them saw it as their duty not to return and to thereby to make a public display of their anti-communist stance.

Despite the initial reaction, eventually over 100,000 – under half of the Poles, did make the choice to return to their native Poland. This number still left the British authorities with the dilemma of managing the remaining Poles following demobilization (there was never any suggestion that the Polish Army would continue in the same form on British soil following the war), and how to effectively feed, re-house, re-train and integrate into British society, a growing number of immigrants (and their families) without destabilizing her social life and institutions.

To address these problems, The Polish Resettlement Corps (PRC) (*Polski Korpus Przysposobienia I Rozmieszczenia*) was formed in May 1946. It was set-up as a Corps of the British Army and had as its aim to enable the demobilization – over a two-year period, of over 100,000 Polish soldiers, sailors and airmen who wished to remain in Britain, and to ease their transition from a Polish military environment to civilian life. Other organizations such as the Polish Assistance Board and the Committee for the Education of the

A scene at Tilbury docks: on the dockside, the Guards band entertains thousands of Polish troops on board SS *BANFORA*, moored alongside, as they wait to depart from Britain, 31 December 1945. Many of them would face prosecution at the hands of communist regime for serving alongside the Western Allies.

From the Imperial War Museum Collection of images of the REPATRIATION OF POLISH SERVICEMEN FROM BRITAIN TO POLAND, 1945-1948
Image supplied under license © Imperial War Museum (D26811) LIC-15996-V8Q5B9

Poles, were also formed to assist in this undertaking. Legislation in the form of the Polish Resettlement Bill 1947 was brought before parliament to support these initiatives and to provide the framework that would provide legislation to enable the Poles to eventually receive Health Service, pension and other forms of benefit entitlements.

These measures also provided for the use of over 200 Polish Resettlement Camps. Wooden and Nissen-hut accommodation within former military camps located in remote locations throughout Britain would later house just under a quarter of a million Poles. Some, like *Jerzy*, were able to obtain assistance and alternative temporary accommodation through contacts they had in Britain and/or because their knowledge of English was good enough for them to make their own housing and living arrangements. Some 130,00 Poles would additionally leave Poland to come to England in the years immediately following the end of the war. My stepfather, was a case in point. *Witold Pomykaj* left Poland having spent the war as a member of the Polish Home Army. After liberation by the allies from a concentration camp in Germany, *Witold* obtained a scholarship to Oxford university where he was able to complete his law studies and eventually to settle in Britain.

From March 1948, The Home Office announced that applications from Polish ex-servicemen could be made for British Citizenship. Although *Jerzy* did not choose to relinquish his Polish nationality, his children – *Theresa, Konstanty* and *Anita*, did later become naturalized British subjects.

For some, adapting to life in Britain also involved a change of name, as for many English-speakers the pronunciation or spelling of Polish names was often next to impossible. For instance, in the case of Captain *Wiesław SZCZYGIET*, his title was conveniently reduced to Captain '*SHIGEL*'[3]. *Stefan KWIATKOWSKI*, became known as *Stefan 'KAY'*[4]. *Jerzy* was soon used to being called '*George*' (a direct translation from Polish to English of *Jerzy*) and his son, my uncle, would later drop the use of *Konstanty* as his first name in favor of one of his middle names – Andrew ('*Andrzej*'); he never, under any circumstances, used his other middle name – *Adolf*.

During 1946, *Jerzy* visited his sister-in-law, *Gabriela*, a nun at the convent of *Blanche de Castille* on the outskirts of *Lille* in northern France. Using her help and calling upon the incredible number of acquaintances and contacts whom she had made from all walks of life in Poland, France and in England, arrangements were made for his wife *Maria* and the children to be removed from Poland to join *Jerzy* in England.

When *Jerzy* said goodbye to his wife in 1939, it had already been decided between them that **Warsaw**, before long, would not be safe and that *Maria* was to return with the children to their country home at the first opportunity. Thereafter, having spent most of the war at **Radostów**, as attacks by bandits became commonplace in and around the areas of south-eastern Poland during 1946, *Maria* took the children and a maid to the safety of a flat belonging to friends at *Narutowicza* Street in **Hrubieszów**. Despite the up-heaval, the maid running off and *Maria*'s almost non-existent domestic skills, food did reach the table and arrangement were even put in place for the children to continue some semblance of schooling.

Konstanty, Jerzy's son, would recall how one day in July 1946 while at the family flat in **Hrubieszów** with his mother and sister (*Anita*), a messenger delivered a telegram to the house. The message, simply signed with the letter 'J', instructed *Maria* to go immediately to a certain hotel in **Warsaw**. Hoping, praying, and even daring to presume that the telegram had been sent by *Jerzy* – from whom she had only heard a few words since the beginning of the war – *Maria* swiftly arranged for a neighbor to look after the girls. When *Theresa*, her eldest daughter, returned from school, *Maria* left the flat with *Konstanty* to catch the next train to **Warsaw**.

Konstanty recalled that the locomotive pulling the train that day was preceded by two empty wagons – a precaution against mines that were frequently left on the tracks. The train eventually pulled into **Warsaw** late in the afternoon. The sights that greeted *Konstanty* made a lasting impression upon him and he later remembered how the city had been reduced to rubble and yet was teeming with people. He remembered seeing a temporary bridge constructed from timber decking, secured onto small boats that were lashed together. This make-shift pontoon was the only way for pedestrians to cross the River **Vistula**. He and his mother took a *dorożka* (a horse-drawn cart) from the train station to the outskirts of **Warsaw**, where they spent the night with *Janina, Jerzy*'s sister, who had left **Radostów** and was by then living in their small flat in the city. At the time, images of war-torn **Warsaw** gave the impression that people were going about their lives as if the war had not yet stopped (see Andrzej Wajda's "*Ashes and Diamonds*"). Indeed, to a certain extent "the Polish underground" was still operational.

The following morning, *Maria* and *Janina* made their way to the hotel as directed in the telegram. They stood outside the hotel for a while, not really knowing what to expect. Suddenly, a complete stranger appeared from nowhere and introduced himself. Following a brief exchange of cordial formalities, it became apparent to *Maria* that she would not be seeing *Jerzy* after all. Rather, the stranger explained that he had received instructions from *Jerzy* to take *Maria* and the children from Poland without delay to safety in France. For the time being she had only managed to bring *Konstanty* with her to **Warsaw** – *Theresa* and *Anita*, her two daughters, were still in **Hrubieszów** and whichever way it was arranged, it would take a number of days to bring the girls back to the city. The decision was made to return *Konstanty* to the same hotel the following afternoon and that he alone would join the – for want of a better word – 'people smuggler' for the journey out of Poland. Other arrangements would have to be put in place in respect of *Maria* and the girls.

On the afternoon of 13 July 1946, *Konstanty* said farewell to his mother as he embarked on a long journey with someone who had been introduced to him as an 'uncle'. *Maria*, in the meantime returned to **Hrubieszów**.

Within a few hours **Konstanty** found himself in the back of a lorry with about twelve other adults whom he had never met before, evidently heading for the Czechoslovak border. After a march through a forest that lasted all night, several more days of walking and a ride by train in a cattle car, on 12 August 1946 and four weeks after leaving **Warsaw**, *Konstanty* arrived in Lille in northern France. To his delight, he was once again reunited with his father who had made his way there from Scotland. *Jerzy* stayed with his son in the convent at *Blanche de Castille* for a few days while *Konstanty* got to know his aunt, *Gabriela* (affectionately known as *'Ciocia Benia'*). This was also an opportunity for *Jerzy* to somehow revise the plan for *Maria* and their two daughters to leave Poland, in such a way so as not to alert the authorities there.

On 22 August, *Jerzy* left his son in the care of the nuns at the convent and returned to Scotland.

Gabriela Breza (*Ciocia 'Benia'*) *Jerzy's* sister-in-law, in the former habit of the Order of the Soeurs du Saint-Enfant Jésus
France c1940

Over the months that followed, with *Gabriela's* help, *Maria* found a position as a translator in a small factory in *Lille* in France, that had been employing a large workforce of exiled Poles – many of whom were unable to speak French. (*Maria* spoke the language fluently.) The paperwork that would satisfy the Polish authorities that she was not leaving Poland permanently, would now have to be drawn-up with the help of her father – Count *Breza*, back in Poland. Permits were eventually obtained and, on 3 October 1947, *Maria*, *Theresa* and *Anita* crossed the Polish border by train into Czechoslovakia, eventually arriving in Lille in France where they were reunited with *Jerzy* and son *Konstanty*. It was the first time that the family had been together since September 1939, eight years previously. In the meantime, *Gabriela* – through people whom she had met in England, was able to secure a place for *Konstanty* at a boarding school in Hertfordshire. *Jerzy* and *Maria* would now travel with him to England and moved into a rented flat in Lordship Road in London's Stoke Newington. *Theresa* and *Anita* remained at the convent at *Blanche de Castille* on the outskirts of *Lille* to complete their Baccalaureate.

At around this time *Jerzy* started to develop unexplained pains in his lower back. He progressively started losing the use of his legs and was unable to walk without the aid of a stick. In an effort to determine what was wrong, he was admitted to hospital in London between 10 May 1948 and 3 June 1948 although tests that he underwent were inconclusive and only a non-specific neurological condition could be identified.

Later that year, *Maria* had their second son, *George*, born in 1948 and the family moved to larger accommodation, first at Stanhope Lane in London's borough of Finchley, and then to Braemar Avenue in Wimbledon, a suburb of south London.

On 6 October 1948, having been declared totally disabled, *Jerzy* relinquished his commission in the Polish Resettlement Corps. By then he had become virtually housebound. Responding to an advertisement in the Polish newspaper – the '*Dziennik Polski*', (still in print today) the family moved to Dukes Avenue, Muswell Hill in north London where they rented the top floor of a small terraced house. Their landlord, who lived with his wife downstairs, was none other than the former Polish Col. *Kazimierz Rumsza*, who had also settled with his family in London after the war.

Jerzy, Polish Resettlement Corps, London 1946

(Right to Left: *Jerzy* reunited with the family for the first time since 1939, standing beside *Maria*, son *Konstanty*, daughters *Anita* and *Theresa* with *Gabriela* (*Ciocia Benia*)

Convent of *Blanche de Castille, Lille*, France 1947

DISCHARGE OF ALIENS: IDENTITY CERTIFICATE.

This certificate will be issued to the soldier when he leaves the unit or hospital on discharge or on terminal furlough pending discharge or on release from Army service.
A copy of this certificate will be despatched to the O. i/c Records concerned.

I hereby certify that the bearer, No. *P/4763*   Rank *CAPT.*

Full Name *DOBIECKI. J. S.*   Nationality *Polish*
(Block Capitals)

NO. 50 OFFICERS HOLDING UNIT.
of the *P.R.C.* KINGWOOD COMMON CAMP,   is proceeding on *30.9.48*
(Regiment or Corps)   HENLEY-ON-THAMES, OXON.   (Date)

from ....

POLISH
47 5

address at *BRAEMAR AVE, WIMBLEDON PARK, LONDON*
(Full Postal Address *S.W.19*

†on leave pending his discharge from the Army *Completion of Contract*
†Strike out on his discharge from the Army. *Relinquished*
whichever is †on relegation to Class W or W(T) of the Reserve.
inapplicable †on leave pending transfer/transfer/to /Class Z or Z(T) of the Reserve.

He has been instructed to report to the police on his arrival in *LONDON*
His Police Registration Book, if held by the O. i/c Records concerned, will be sent to him within the course of the next few days.

No. 50 OFFICERS HOLDING
UNIT
27 SEP 1948

UNIT-STAMP.

Signature ....
Station ....
Date *28.9.48*

(32291) Wt.31955/1131   19,000   12/46   A. & E.W.Ltd.   Gp.698
(32700) Wt.38800/1457   125,000 12/46   "   "

Discharge certificate – Capt. *Jerzy* Dobiecki
Issued 28.09.1948 on completion of service with the Polish Resettlement Corps
Image courtesy of The National Archives

Tel. Godalming 1520 ext /32

 ͻ ͻ ͻ ͻ ͻ/0/1249/48.

P.R.C. - O.F. 87.

POLISH RESETTLEMENT CORPS /ATS POLISH RESETTLEMENT SECTION/.
RELINQUISHMENT OF COMMISSION.   5A

    The undermentioned officer has ceased service with the Polish Resettlement Corps /ATS Polish Resettlement Section/ and his/her commission is to be relinquished. Will you therefore arrange the necessary action.

/a/ PRC. No. POLISH/. **4763.**

/b/ SURNAME /Block letters/ ..... **DOBIECKI**

/c/ CHRISTIAN NAME/S/ /Block letters/ **JERZY, STANISŁAW**

/d/ Local Rank ..... **CAPT.**

/e/ Date commission is to be relinquished ..... **30. 9. 48.**

/f/ Date officers was commissioned into Polish Resettlement Corps
/ATS/Polish Resettlement Section/ ..... **1. 10. 46.**

                                                 RELINQUISHMENT OF COMMISSION

/g/ Reason for officers ceasation of service .....
    ON COMPLETION OF CONTRACT.

/h/ Present home address of officer ..... **LONDON, S.W. 19**
1. BRAEMAR AVE. WIMBLEDON PARK

Witley Camp,
Godalming,

Date ..... **6. 10. 48.**

DISTRIBUTION.
War Office /A.G.1./Officers R/
W.O. Polish Resettlement Corps.

                                 2Lt
                      FOR Colonel,
        O.i/C. P.R.C. Record Office.

101/2

Military correspondence confirming discharge of Capt. *Jerzy* Dobiecki
Issued 06.10.1948 on completion of service with the Polish Resettlement Corps
Image courtesy of The National Archives

CHAPTER 10
EXILE IN ENGLAND
(1948-1958)

By 1952, his youngest son, *George,* remembers that *Jerzy* would suddenly and on numerous occasions fall to the floor without warning. As his condition worsened, *Jerzy* was unable to walk, became confined to bed and had to make numerous lengthy stays in hospital, including admission as an in-patient at the Mabledon Hospital in Kent, south east England. The hospital housed a neurosis unit that was managed and staffed by Polish doctors and nurses providing treatment and support for approximately 200 Polish ex-servicemen who were receiving care and psychiatric help for a range of conditions caused by the effects of the war. *George* recalls travelling by bus with his mother from north London to London Bridge railway station, and by train to Dartford in Kent in order to see his father at the Mabledon unit. He remembers his mother buying bangles and a small trinket from one of the longer-term Polish patients there, who had used his skills to make small items of jewelry as part of his rehabilitation.

Following a number of operations to alleviate the increasingly excruciating cramps in his legs, *Jerzy* died in hospital on Wednesday, 26 November 1958. He was aged 63. It was confirmed that his death was due to 'Disseminated Sclerosis' (more commonly known today as Multiple Sclerosis).

Jerzy was a soldier for over half his life, serving with distinction in three different armies that had engaged in three wars. He never met all of his grandchildren or his great grandchildren, was unable to return to his native Poland following the war or to witness Poland's restoration to a fully independent, thriving, democratic nation that later joined the European Union. As Jerzy's lasting legacy, he leaves his first-hand testimony of events that befell Poland during both the Polish war with Russia from 1919 to 1921 and the Second World War between 1939 and 1945.

In recognition of his services to Poland Jerzy was awarded:

(From the Authorities in Poland):

Krzyż Walecznych ....(The Cross of Valour)
Srebrny Krzyż Zasługi ....(The Silver Cross of Merit)
Medal za Wojnę 1918-1921 ....(1918-1921 War Medal)
Brązowy Medal za Długoletnią Służbę .... (Long Service Medal)
Medal 10-lecia Odzyskanej Niepodległości ... (Medal marking ten years of
Independence)

(From the Authorities in Great Britain):

The 1939-1945 War Medal

Jerzy's main family home at **Radostów** was never re-built after its destruction during the First World War; today none of the original buildings or other structures remain – and the land that used to form part of the estate languishes in the possession of the State.

During the 20 years of the 18th Polish Pomeranian Lancers Regiment's existence, it had 8 Commanders:

- Col. *August Brochwicz-Donimirski*,   29.05.1919 – 03.11.1920
- Col. *Rudolf Alzner*,   09.11.1920 – 01.07.1922
- Col. *Michał Ostrowski*,   01.07.1922 – 01.05.1923
- Col. *Stefan Jacek Dembiński*,   01.05.1923 – 28.01.1928
- Col. *Albert Traeger*,   28.01.1928 – 01.05.1932
- Col. *Kazimierz Kosiarski*,   01.05.1932 – 01.02.1938
- Col. *Tadeusz Kurnatowski*,   01.02.1938 – 01.08.1939
- Col. *Kazimierz Mastalerz*,   01.08.1939 – 01.09.1939

The deputy commanders were:

- Major *Lewalt-Jezierski*   July 1920 – March 1921
- Lt. Col. *Jerzy Dembicki*,   March 1921 – Nov. 1922
- Lt. Col. *Stefan Jacek Dembiński*,   Nov. 1922 – May 1923
- Lt. Col. Kazimierz Ziembiński,   May 1923 – March 1925
- Major *Józef Koczwara*,   March 1925 – Jan. 1930
- Major *Ludomir Wysocki*,   Jan. 1930 – Jan. 1931
- Major *Marian Ossowski*,   Jan. 1931 – Jan. 1934
- Major *Jan Małysiak*,   Jan. 1934 – July 1938
- Lt. Col. *Eugeniusz Chrzanowski*,   July 1938 – Aug. 1939
- Major *Stanisław Malecki*,   Aug. 1939 – Sept. 1939

In September 1939, the 18th Polish Pomeranian Lancers Regiment lost:

- 17 officers

- 9 officer cadets

- 3 NCOs

- 36 troopers.

Thirteen officers connected to the regiment were subsequently murdered in the Katyn massacre.

In September 1939, in recognition of the courage and dedication shown by the regiment, Gen. *Stanisław Grzmot-Skotnicki* decorated the regimental standard with the Silver Cross of the Order of Virtuti Military – Poland's highest military award for bravery.

The standard of the 18th Polish Pomeranian Lancers Regiment was taken by its Ułans to war. During the ensuing battles in 1939, the fabric of the regimental Color was shot- through several times. On 3 September 1939, Platoon Commander *Antoni Osiecki* detached the torn standard from its flagpole, placed it into a leather satchel and buried it in the woods near *Grupa* (53 km north of *Toruń*) and a short distance from the *Świecie – Warlubie* road. This solemn event was witnessed by Maj. *Malecki*, Cavalry Capt. *Retman*, Cavalry Capt. *Godlewski*, Sr. Sgt. *Urban* and several other Ułans of the regiment.

In 1950, acting with the support of the Polish Army Museum, Cavalry Capt. *Wacław Godlewski* led an expedition in an attempt to find the spot where the standard had been hidden. Unfortunately, the topography of the area where it was believed to have been buried had changed so much that the mission was unsuccessful. The colors were never recovered.

A replacement for the standard was consecrated in May 1982 and today is kept in the Hall of National Remembrance at the 18th Regiment of Pomeranian Lancers Primary School in *Nowa Cerkiew* (approximately 56 km south of *Gdańsk* in northern Poland).

'……. Honor i Ojczyzna…….' (Honor and the Fatherland)
Standard of the 18th Polish Pomeranian Lancers Regiment

(Images reproduced by kind permission of Sławomir Ziętarski 18th Polish
Pomeranian Lancers Regimental Volunteer Association)
© Sławomir Ziętarski

During the 1960s, Maj. *Zygmunt Szpotański* chaired a committee to erect a memorial at the site of the 18th Pomeranian Lancers' last cavalry charge and engagement at **Krojanty**. On 11 September 1966, the memorial was unveiled and during his speech at the ceremony, Brig. Gen. *Roman Abraham*, a former Commander of the Pomeranian Cavalry Brigade, said:

> **"...The chivalry of the Ułans was cut short at Krojanty,**
> **as was our solitary battle that would end in defeat in September 1939;**
> **but there is no defeat that will not ultimately lead to victory..."**

Memorial to the Uhłans of the 18th Polish Pomeranian Lancers Regiment **Krojanty**, Poland

© Panoramio.com

For their part in the war of 1919-1921, 15 Ułans of the 18th Pomeranian Lancers Regiment were awarded Poland's second highest award of the *'Silver Cross of the Order of Virtuti Militari'. Jerzy Dobiecki*, together with 60 Ułans of the regiment were awarded the *'Cross of Valour 1918-1921'* for bravery. The Regimental Day is still celebrated each year in Poland on 29 May – to coincide with the regiment's departure to the Russo-Polish Front on 29 May 1920.

Every year, on the first Sunday of September, a service is held in tribute to those of the regiment who fell in September 1939 and to commemorate the 18th Pomeranian Lancers' charge at **Krojanty.**

In 2006, *Jerzy's* remains, together with those of *Maria,* were transferred from Highgate cemetery in London – where both had originally been buried, to their final resting place in the *Dobiecki* family tomb at the *Powązki* Cemetery in **Warsaw.**

Jerzy and *Maria*, London 1951

(left to right)

Jerzy von Heintze with wife *Theresa* (my father and mother) with *Anita* and husband *Stanisław Milewski*, London 1958

Konstanty ('Andy') Dobiecki with *Gabriela Breza ('Ciocia Benia')*
England 1958

George Dobiecki,
Our Lady of Muswell Catholic Primary
school,
London 1958

APPENDICES

APPENDIX ONE

Timeline of events in Polish/European history between 1795 and 2016

APPENDIX ONE

Timeline of Polish/European history between 1795 and 2016

The Commonwealth of Poland and Lithuania, also known as the 'Kingdom of Poland and Lithuania', prior to its later partition in the 18th century, had joined together the independent Kingdom of Poland and neighboring Grand Duchy of Lithuania by numerous Acts of Union since the end of the fourteenth century. At the start of the 1600s this Commonwealth was one of the largest countries in Europe with territory that included present-day Poland, Ukraine, Belarus, Lithuania, Latvia, much of Estonia, parts of Russia, and sections of Moldova and of Romania. Over time, with political developments as they were in Europe during the eighteenth century, the engagement by the Commonwealth in several wars, a progressive reduction in the size of its army and insolvency of the banks in *Warsaw* following a general decline in economic activity[1], all contributed towards a greatly weakened Commonwealth and one that was unable to withstand the expansionist foreign policy of its three neighboring empires. Over the course of three 'Partitions' in 1772, 1793 and finally in 1795, the Commonwealth was gradually divided entirely between Prussia, Austria and Russia. Each empire imposed its own legal, judicial, monetary, educational and administrative systems on the Polish and Lithuanian lands, introducing extensive censorship and, certainly in the case of Poland, attempted in varying degrees to abolish both the Polish language and to suppress the country's very cultural identity. Decisions of what was to happen in the former Polish territories were taken in Berlin, Vienna and St Petersburg.[2] Poland as a 'State' effectively ceased to exist on the political map of Europe[3] and did not return as a sovereign entity until 1918, over one hundred years later.

Although only limited detail of the impact that Polish culture had upon the Polish struggle during this period is included in the timeline that follows, mention has to be made of the richness of the country's cultural activities that played such an enormous part in sustaining the Poles during their seemingly never-ending struggle for independence. The essence of Polish identity survived despite the ethnic, regional and religious differences of the different peoples of Poland, together with the numerous attempts over the centuries to subject so many Polish communities to the ways and laws of three very different and opposing foreign empires. Catholicism along with Polish literature, art, music and theatre provided much of the 'glue' that enabled the Poles to not only feel unified in a common resolve to overcome the injustices that they were subjected to over so many years, but helped to keep alive – through reminiscences of the past – an inextinguishable spirit of hope. At roughly the time that Jerzy was born, Polish literature towards the end of the nineteenth century saw the emergence of some of Poland's greatest authors such as *Józef Ignacy Kraszewski* (1812-1887) who popularized the history and life of the Polish nation. *Aleksander Głowacki* (1845-1912), to many was regarded as Poland's Charles Dickens and wrote about the moral and social maladies of the day. *Eliza Orzeszkowa* (1841-1910) wrote about various social classes and *Henryk Sienkiewicz* (1846-1916) produced inspired tales of the Polish struggle, went on to receive the Nobel Prize for Literature and joined the ranks of the world's greatest writers.

1795   As the Polish-Lithuanian Commonwealth lands are annexed by Prussia, Austria and Russia (Russia took over 62% of Polish territory[4]), King *Stanisław II August Poniatowski* (1732-1798), King of Poland and Grand Duke of Lithuania, abdicates.

1797   In the hope of one day liberating and restoring Poland[5], 6,000[6] Poles join the French army and subsequently fight as part of the Polish legions, in French Service, fighting in the French campaign against Italy.[7] During the six years of the formation of three Polish legions, approximately 25,000 Poles passed through their ranks.[8]

  Józef Wybicki (1747-1822), émigré politician striving for the independence of Poland, writes the words to the "Song of the Polish legions in Italy" later to be adopted as the official Polish national anthem in 1926.

  'Denisko' Uprising in *Podole* and *Pokucie* regions of former Polish Commonwealth, (so named after *Joachim Denisko* (1756-1812).

  Death of Catherine the Great.

1801   Alexander I (1777-1825) becomes Russian Tsar.

1803   Opening of Polish University of *Wilno* (**Vilnius**).

1804   Napoleon Bonaparte crowned "Emperor of the French"; commences campaign of wars in Europe.

1805   Napoleon's 'Grande Armée' defeats Austro-Russian armies at *Austerlitz* (The battlefield is located in the modern-day Czech Republic, which at the time was part of the Austrian empire).

1806   Following the defeat of the Prussian Army at the Battles of *Jena* and *Auerstedt* in Saxony (present-day Germany), the French army forces the retreating Prussian and Russian armies across Polish territory.

French troops enter **Warsaw** in November.

Polish Gen. *Jan Dąbrowski* (1755-1818) is at the head of Polish legions in Napoleon's army.

Subsequent battles between the French and the retreating armies are fought on Polish soil at: *Biezut, Czarnowo, Kołozqb, Soldan, Pułtusk* and *Gołymin.*

Holy Roman Empire is superseded by 'Austrian' Empire.[9]

1807 Napoleon continues his advance on Russia, defeating the Russian army at the Battle of *Friedland* (formerly Prussia, today part of a Russian exclave surrounded by Poland and Lithuania).

Under the Treaties of *Tilsit,* Polish territory originally taken by Prussia formed into the Duchy of **Warsaw** (central and eastern parts of present - day Poland and parts of Lithuania and Belarus).

King *Frederick August of Saxony* appointed by Napoleon to become the Grand Duke of **Warsaw**.

Sejm (parliament) retains responsibility for passing legislation – now in line with the Napoleonic Code.

Abolition of serfdom in the Duchy of **Warsaw**.[10]

Formation of a regular, conscripted army in the Duchy comprising over 30,000 men.[11] The Duchy's Ułans ('Lancers') later became a model for lancer regiments of many European armies.[12]

Introduction of 6-year conscription for every man in the Duchy between 21 and 28 years of age.[13]

1809 Austria attempts to retake Duchy of **Warsaw** but is defeated at the Battle of *Raszyn* by Polish Militia led by *Józef Poniatowski* (1763- 1813).

At the subsequent Treaty of Vienna, the region of Galicia is ceded to the Duchy from Austria.

1810   Birth of *Fryderyk Chopin* (1810-1849) in *Żelazowa Wola*, in what was then the Duchy of **Warsaw**.

1812   In the hope of fighting for the restoration and eventual independence of Poland, 100,000[14] Poles join Napoleon's army that marches across Europe to Moscow during the Franco-Russian War. Despite notable engagements at *Smolensk* and *Borodino*, the Campaign ends in disaster for the French. An estimated 72,000 Poles are lost.[15]

1813   Death of *Józef Poniatowski,* now Marshal in Napoleon's army, together with great numbers of Poles, at the Battle of *Leipzig* during Napoleon's Campaign against the coalition of empires – seeking to wrest German states from French control.

1815   Following Napoleon's defeat at the Battle of *Waterloo* (in modern-day Belgium), Congress of Vienna agrees a solution to the balance of power in Europe, in an effort to end 25 years of conflict.

The majority of the Duchy of **Warsaw** is given to Russia and renamed the **Congress Kingdom of Poland** with the Russian Tsar, Alexander I as king.

Remainder of the former Duchy is formed into the Grand Duchy of *Posen* (roughly equivalent in size to modern-day Belgium[16]) and ceded to Prussia.

Kraków becomes a 'free city' – a joint Protectorate of Austria, Prussia and Russia.

Henceforth, **Congress Kingdom of Poland** is integrated politically with Russia.

This period is generally seen as one of relative stability and economic growth for the region.[17]

Establishment of a Polish army of 30,000 soldiers.[18]

1816   University of **Warsaw** founded.[19]

1817   First steam engine to be used anywhere in the former Kingdom is installed in **Kraków**.[20]

Attempts to eradicate Polish culture continue in areas taken over by the three Empires; Polish villages go on strike in *Masuria* in eastern Prussia (modern-day northern Poland).

1824   Constitution for the Grand Duchy of *Posen* formally proclaimed.

Gdańsk region of *Pomerania* (northwest Poland) made a Prussian province.

Polish landed estates taken over by new German owners in *Poznań* area.

1825   Death of Tsar Alexander I.

1826   One of the first sugar refineries established in Poland.[21]

1828   Foundation of the Polish Bank.[22]

1829   Nicholas I (1796-1855), Tsar Emperor of Russia, crowned as the King of Congress Kingdom of Poland in *Warsaw* cathedral.[23]

1830   Period of worsening economic crisis and widespread unemployment.[24]

Unrest spreads through Congress Kingdom of Poland, sparking a military revolt. Insurrection spreads to western Russian provinces.

Unrest coincides with the 'Second Revolution' in France.

National uprising called by the *Sejm* and proclamation of the dethronement of the Russian Tsar.

Period of the 'Great Emigration'.

Period also known as the 'November Uprising' or 'Polish-Russian War 1830-1831'.

Gen. *Józef Chłopicki* (1798-1845) assumes dictatorial powers.

Adam Czartoryski (1770-1861) forms a new Polish government.

Prince *Michał Radziwiłł* (1778-1850) nominated Commander-in-Chief of the army, now numbering 80,000 soldiers.[25]

1831   Russian army marches into Congress Kingdom of Poland. Over the course of 325 days[26] and following a number of battles, Polish forces are defeated.

Tsar dismantles Polish government and having lost its sovereignty, the constitution of the Congress Kingdom of Poland is suspended and the territory is placed directly under rule of the Russian Empire.

Polish army is abolished.[27]

Martial law is imposed. 10,000 Poles emigrate[28], including kingdom's political, military and cultural elite.[29] Polish Émigré communities in France and Britain foster nostalgia for the lost homeland. Large numbers of noble families are deported or forced to re-settle in Russia, their manors confiscated.[30] Over 2,540 manors are sequestrated, 80,000 Poles deported to Russia, 254 political and military leaders condemned to death.[31]

Polish mood of the time particularly expressed in works by *Chopin, Mickiewicz* and others.

1834 The poet *Adam Mickiewicz* (1798-1855) publishes his epic work about country life in Lithuania, entitled '*Pan Tadeusz*'.

1840 One of the first sugar beet refineries in Kingdom of Poland is founded by *Tytus Wojciechowski* (1808-1879) in **Poturzyn,** south-eastern Poland.[32]

Lithuanian legal code replaced by Russian law.[33]

1841 Polish *złoty* withdrawn from circulation, replaced with the *ruble*.[34]

1846 Riots and demonstrations in the city of **Kraków** lead to an armed revolt that is suppressed by Russian and Austrian troops; the ensuing Austro- Russian Treaty ceded **Kraków** to the Austrian empire and the Austrian Emperor becomes its Duke.

1848 Spread of revolutionary sentiment throughout Europe after Paris mob overthrows the French regime of *Louis Philippe*; hardly a state in Europe is not affected by disturbances[35] ('Springtime of Nations') that manifest themselves in Congress Kingdom of Poland as an unsuccessful military insurrection by the Poles against Prussia.

Grand Duchy of Posen abolished as territory becomes a Prussian province.

Abolition of serfdom in the Polish lands forming part of the Austrian Empire.[36]

Martial law imposed in Austrian Poland until 1854.[37]

Completion of the **Warsaw**-Vienna Railway.[38]

1850	Large scale development of industry continues as the Industrial Revolution across the three empires progresses at different paces.[39]
1854	Russian defeat in the Crimean War against Britain, France and Turkey which had challenged Russian ambitions in the Balkans.
1855	Death of Tsar Nicholas. Succeeded by Tsar Alexander II (1818-1881) who imposes political and cultural measures that coincides with a further period of economic growth.[40]
1858	Martial law originally imposed on Polish Kingdom by Russia in 1831 is lifted.
1860	Violent unrest and protest marches against Russian rule in **Warsaw**.
1861	Martial law re-established in **Warsaw**.
	Abolition of serfdom in the Russian Empire.
1863	Despite facing overwhelming military odds, the start of sixteen-month insurrection/guerrilla war against Tsarist tyranny ('The January Uprising').
	Proclamation by the Temporary National Government that calls for an abolition of serfdom and liberation of Polish lands.
	Fighting throughout Polish Kingdom, Belarus and Lithuania intensifies.
1864	Martial Law imposed across Congress Kingdom of Poland as Austrian, Russian and Prussian governments quell the insurrection.
	Serfdom is abolished in Russian-held Polish lands.[41]
	Administrative system in Congress Kingdom of Poland integrated with the rest of the Russian Empire, the Congress Kingdom is effectively dissolved.
	Start of program of intensive imposition of Russian policies over Polish territory: strikes prohibited, prohibition of

land-purchase by Poles.

Russian language imposed as the language of civic administration, secondary schools and of the courts.

50,000[42] Poles sent to Siberia during period of intense repression.[43]

Tsar relinquishes duties as King of Congress Kingdom of Poland which is dissolved and henceforth *Warsaw* becomes capital of the *Privislinskiy Kray* or *Vistulaland*[44] as the name 'Poland' is formally abolished.

1867	Austro-Hungarian Empire formed.
1869	Russian language imposed on the University of *Warsaw*.
1872	German language imposed on schooling in Prussian Poland.[45]
1876	German language imposed as the official language in all Polish provinces under the control of the Berlin Government.[46]
1879	For the Polish territories falling within the tsarist empire, Russian becomes mandatory in the teaching of all secondary schools.[47] The church effectively becomes the only place where Polish is allowed to be spoken in public.
1881	Assassination of Tsar Alexander II in *St Petersburg*.
1894	Accession of Tsar Nicholas II (1868-1918), the last Tsar of Russia.
1895	***Birth of Jerzy Dobiecki in Poturzyn, south-east Poland***.
1899	Outbreak of fire at the Wojciechowski sugar beet refinery in *Poturzyn*.[48]
1903	*Maria Curie-Skłodowska* (1867-1934) awarded Nobel Prize for Physics.
1904	Attack by Japan on the Russian fleet in Manchuria gives rise to renewed anti-Russian sentiment in Poland.[49]
1905	Unrest and strikes spread through Russia in protest of the regime.

Following the 'Bloody Sunday' demonstration in *St Petersburg*, revolution/civil war in the Russian Empire spreads to Russian-controlled Poland with insurrections at *Łódź* and *Warsaw*.

Martial law imposed on the Vistulaland.

Henryk Sienkiewicz (1846-1916) awarded Nobel Prize for Literature.

1908   Rise in Polish and Ukrainian nationalism.

With tacit approval of the Austrian authorities, a Polish army of about 10,000 men[50], under the guise of sporting clubs and a Riflemen's Union, jointly known as the *'Union for Active Resistance'* is founded by *Kazimierz Sosnkowski* (1885-1969) and *Władysław Sikorski* (1881- 1943).

1910   Foreseeing the possibility of a future war, *Józef Piłsudski* (1867-1935) enhances the small, part-time Polish armed units – reorganizing them along military lines as part of the Austro-Hungarian army; these units would eventually be turned into 'Polish Legions'[51] of about 20,000 men[52] under the command of Austrian army officers of Polish origin.

1911   *Maria Curie-Skłodowska* obtains a second Nobel Prize (for Chemistry).

1912-1913   Balkan Wars lead to defeat of forces of the Ottoman Empire but leave tensions and territorial ambitions of countries in the area unresolved.

1914 - 1919   Outbreak of *The Great War*, August 1914, borne out of German rivalry with France, Britain and Russia and the dispute between Austria- Hungary and Serbia.[53] The origins of the war were underpinned by colonial, naval and coalition tensions between these countries[54] and as conflict spread beyond the three partitioning powers across Europe, the Middle East, Africa and Asia this was once again seen by Poles as an opportunity for the resurrection of an independent, sovereign Polish State.[55]

Hundreds of thousands[56] of Poles mobilized as part of the armies of the three occupying powers (Russian, Austro-Hungarian and German) as Germany and Austria-Hungary (the 'Central Powers') wage war against Russia and its allies – France and Britain (the 'Entente').[57]

Formation of Polish legions in Austrian, Russian and German armies.[58]

Russian army advances and retreats over Polish land in confrontations with German and Austro-Hungarian forces.

Restoration of **Kingdom of Poland** by Germany[59] that occupies Poland.

German military rule introduced in Kingdom of Poland (1915).

Polish National Committee established in Switzerland (1917)[60] (a Polish government in exile) which then moves to Paris.[61]

Restoration of Poland's sovereignty listed in US President *Woodrow Wilson*'s 14-Point Plan of US war aims.

Russia undergoes two revolutions in 1917 resulting in the overthrow of the Romanov dynasty. Government is replaced by the communist Bolshevik regime under *Vladimir Lenin* (1870-1924).

Russian Republic renamed the 'Russian Soviet Federative Socialist Republic' on 10 July 1918. Russian army dissolved, and Russia withdraws from the war.

An armistice ends hostilities of the Great War in 1918.

Regency Council set up in **Warsaw**, power handed to *Józef Piłsudski* who becomes Chief of State and Commander-in-Chief of Polish armed forces.

Ignacy Paderewski (1860-1941) becomes first democratically elected Prime Minister following the Declaration of the Independence of the Republic of Poland on November 11 1918 ('The Second Polish Republic').

Staging of The Paris Peace Conference in 1919. Austro-Hungarian Empire is dismantled.

The Treaty of Versailles recognizes the already renamed **Republic of Poland**'s independence. Former annexed territory is returned to her. Access is once again given to the Baltic Sea. However, the border between Republic of Poland and its eastern neighbors remains in dispute as occupying German forces remain on Polish soil.

Although figures vary, a total of approximately 16 million[62] people perished in the Great War. In Poland, approximately 450,000[63] Poles were killed and about 900,000 were wounded whilst fighting for the Russian, Prussian and Austrian armies.

Industry was paralyzed, communications had been ruptured, agricultural production had fallen dramatically, and poverty was rife.

1918 - 1921 Series of border wars fought by Republic of Poland against:
(1)Newly formed Republic of Czechoslovakia (1919-1920)
(2)The West Ukrainian Peoples' Republic (1918-1919)
(3) Lithuania (1919-1920)
(4) Russia (1919-1921).
(5) Germany (1918-1919)
(6) Germany (over Silesia) (1919-1921)

Military Draft announced in Republic of Poland to face the Bolshevik offensive – an advancing Red Army taking the place of the retreating German forces.

Polish forces expel Bolsheviks from **Vilnius** and **Minsk** (1919).

Polish-Ukrainian Alliance formed, which fails against Bolshevik Russia (1920).

Ukrainian nationalists wage underground war against Polish State.

Although 'Curzon Line' is accepted in Republic of Poland as the demarcation between the Republic and neighboring Russia, Bolshevik forces continue their advance into the Polish Republic.

Battle of **Warsaw** and subsequent rout of the Russian army (1920) during Russo-Polish War, leads to decisive victory for Polish Forces under Marshal *Piłsudski,* halting the 'Red' Army advance into central Europe and thus arresting the intended spread of communism to Europe (also known as the 'Miracle of the Vistula').

Seen as the last great cavalry battle in modern European history, involving 20,000 horsemen on each side, Russian forces were destroyed at *Komarów* near **Zamość**[64].

1920 Foundation of the Geneva-based League of Nations.

Walther Hermann Nernst (1864-1941) awarded Nobel Prize for Chemistry.

1921 Confirmation of gains for Polish Republic of territory in Belarus and western Ukraine although tensions would continue in these former Russian territories, home to large numbers of non-ethnic Poles.

Similar situation arose in former Prussian city of *Danzig* (*Gdańsk*) on the Baltic coast which contained a majority German population.

Polish foreign policy in the region criticized by Britain at the time.[65]

New Constitution voted-in (bi-cameral parliament composed of the *Sejm* and the Senate).

Republic of Poland's population estimated at the time as 27 million.[66]

Treaty of Riga with Bolshevik Russia[67], ending the Russo-Polish War.

1922   *Gabriel Narutowicz* (1865-1922) sworn-in as first President of the Polish Republic but is assassinated five days later in *Warsaw*.

Replaced by *Stanisław Wojciechowski* (1869-1953).

Russia assumes title of the 'Union of Soviet Socialist Republics' (USSR).

1923   Republic of Poland faces economic crisis.

1924   *Władysław Reymont* (1867-1925) receives Nobel Prize for Literature for his work *Chłopi* ('*Peasants*').

Złoty re-introduced as the Republic of Poland's national currency, replacing the Polish *Mark* that had been in circulation with five other currencies in Poland since 1917.

Death of *Lenin*.

Joseph Stalin (1879-1953) appointed as General Secretary of the Communist Party and ruler of the USSR.

1926   Marshal *Piłsudski*, supported by his legions, stages a coup d'état following inability of the government to deal with the economic difficulties.

President resigns following an armed confrontation in *Warsaw*. *Ignacy Mościcki* (1867-1946) is elected to replace him and remains in office until the fall of Poland in September 1939.

Official adoption of musical composition by *Józef Wybicki* as the Polish national anthem (composed in 1797).

1929   World Economic crisis begins following the financial crash of the American stock market;

The 'Great Depression' hits Republic of Poland.[68]

First Polish delegation sent to London to establish a diplomatic legation.

1930   Marshal *Piłsudski* assumes role of Prime Minister.

1932   Polish-Soviet Treaty of Non-Aggression.[69]

1933   *Adolf Hitler* (1889-1945), of Austrian descent, becomes Chancellor of Germany, head of the Nationalist Socialist German Workers' Party (*Nationalsozialistische Deutsche Arbeiterpartei*).

1934   Italian forces invade Abyssinia (modern-day Ethiopia).

1935   Polish-German Treaty of Non-Aggression.[70]

Irène Curie awarded Nobel Prize for Chemistry.

Death of *Marshal Piłsudski*.

1936   Gen. *Edward Rydz-Śmigły* (1886-1941) becomes Marshal of Republic of Poland (Head of the armed forces).

Civil war breaks-out in Spain.

1937   Japan invades China

1938   In an attempt to unify German-speaking people in Europe (the 'Anschluss'), Germany annexes Austria.

At the Munich Agreement, France, United Kingdom and Italy subsequently appease Germany by agreeing to German takeover of *Sudetenland* – Germanic- speaking border areas of Czechoslovakia.

Republic of Poland sends troops into Czechoslovakia and annexes *Cieszyn*.

<u>1939</u>

Czechoslovakia capitulates in the face of threatened aggression by Germany, which sends in an occupying force.

Italy invades Albania.

Mobilization of German troops close to Polish border.

Agreement signed between Soviet Russia and Germany detailing cooperation in the event of future war ('*Molotov-Ribbentrop Pact*'). The agreement also secretly provides for the partitions of Republic of Poland[71], Romania, Lithuania, Latvia, Estonia and Finland.

Agreement of Mutual Assistance between Republic of Poland, United Kingdom and France.

Biuro Szyfrów (Polish Cypher Bureau) hands-over to British and French authorities, secret work it had been undertaking since 1933 to break the German '*Enigma*' encryption code machine.[72]

Germany terminates the Non-Aggression Treaty with Republic of Poland and demands the return of *Danzig* (**Gdańsk**) (request refused by the Poles).

31 August 1939, following a staged attack by German convicts dressed in Polish uniforms on a radio station at *Gliwice* in Germany, Poland is wrongly accused of launching an unprovoked attack on the Third Reich.[73]

Republic of Poland is invaded by Germany, without warning or declaration of war, in the early hours of 1 September 1939 by air, sea and land.

Poland's land army is made up of about 500,000 men, although not all are mobilized and are hugely outnumbered by the invading German forces.

Britain and France declare war on Germany, honoring a previous commitment to stand-by Poland.

Polish 18th Pomeranian Lancers Regiment confronts infantry of German 20th Motorized Division at *Krojanty*.[74]

9 September, Franco-Polish Military Agreement permitting Polish Forces to be formed and engage in combat on French

soil.

17 September, Soviet Forces invade Polish Republic from the east.

By early October, after heavy human losses and the fall of **Warsaw**, the country is once again occupied by Russia and Germany, partitioned between the two along the dividing line agreed-to by the *Molotov- Ribbentrop Pact* earlier in 1939.[75]

In an attempt to preserve as much of the Polish army as possible and to continue the fight from exile[76], Polish Government and military high command, together with units of Polish army (approx. 100,000 Poles)[77], evacuate Republic of Poland to neighboring Romania and Hungary (many having to face immediate internment).

Władysław Raczkiewicz appointed as President of the Polish government in exile – formed in Paris.[78]

Section of Polish navy leaves the Baltic for the safety of British ports.

1940

Polish army in exile (approx. 50,000 men) formed in France, known as the 10th Cavalry Brigade under Gen. *Stanisław Maczek* (1892- 1994).[79]

Germany invades Denmark, Norway, Luxembourg, Netherlands, Belgium and France.

'Government of the Republic of Poland in Exile' transferred to London (47 Portland Place and other venues) led by Gen. *Władysław Sikorski* who becomes Prime Minister and Commander-in-Chief. (This government, despite developments in communist-led Poland over future years, continues to perform its functions in exile until 1990, convening its Council of Ministers at 43 Eaton Place in London every fortnight).[80]

20,000 Polish soldiers evacuate to Britain after the fall of France.[81]

5 August, Anglo-Polish Agreement providing for Polish military service on UK soil.

Polish army units in Britain regrouped into the 1st Polish Corps formed in Scotland under command of Gen. *Marian Kukiel* (1885-1972) with initial responsibility of defending the Scottish eastern coastline from a possible German attack from Norway.[82]

Polish pilots in action during the Battle of Britain (e.g. The Polish 302 & '303 *Kościuszko*' Squadrons).[83] By 1944, the Polish Air Force made up fourteen squadrons[84] of the RAF.

Approximately 40,000 Polish officers are murdered by the Soviet secret police. Of these, in the region of 4,321[85] corpses of Polish officers were later (1943) discovered at *Katyn* near *Smolensk*.

Catastrophic mass killings of civilians during ensuing Holocaust and vicious atrocities and brutalization of the Polish people of all races by Nazi forces throughout Poland, brought to attention of the outside world by Polish government-in-exile in London.[86]

Polish population additionally terrorized into obedience by Soviet apparatus; up to half a million-people deported from Soviet-occupied territories to Siberia and Soviet Central Asia.[87]

One and a half million Poles forced to work as slave labor in German industry and agriculture.[88]

1941

Germany and other 'Axis' Powers invade Soviet Union and lay siege to Leningrad.

Japan attacks Pearl Harbor. The United States enters the War.

Sikorski-Maisky Agreement signed in Moscow creating a Polish Army in the USSR commanded by Gen. *Władisław Anders* (1892-1970).

1942

Counterattack by Soviet troops in Russia which captures German 6th Army.

Together with other organized forms of opposition, the '*Home Army*' (*Armya Krajowa*, '*AK*') and a non-communist 'Underground State' in Poland are formed with allegiance to the exiled government in London.

Formal creation of the 1st Polish Armored Division in Scotland under Gen. *Maczek*.

Establishment of revived Polish communist party in Nazi-occupied Poland (Polish Worker Party).[89]

1943

Warsaw Ghetto Uprising.

Gen. *Sikorski* requests the Red Cross to investigate the circumstances behind the discovery of murdered Polish officers at the forests of Katyn.[90]

Gen. *Sikorski* killed in an unexplained plane crash off the coast of Gibraltar.

Gen. *Kazimierz Sosnkowski* appointed as replacement Commander- in-Chief.

Stanisław Mikołajczyk (1901-1966) appointed Prime Minister of Polish government-in-exile.

USSR severs diplomatic relations with Polish government-in-exile.[91]

Allied Nations' meeting in Tehran at which future ceding of Polish territory to Soviet Union is discussed.

Operation 'Stirrup' in Cambridge and other exercises in the UK put Polish 1st Polish Armored Division (now comprising 10,214 officers and men[92]) to the test in major trials.

December 1943, first units of Polish 2nd Corps land in Italy.

Start of Polish-Ukrainian civil war which spreads from *Volhynia*.

1944

Polish 2nd Corps under Gen. *Anders* heralded for its part in the taking of *Monte Cassino*.

Allied forces land troops in France on 6th June (The D-Day Landings).

Polish 1st Armored Division and units of the Canadian army, having re-located to Aldershot from bases in Scotland, land in France on the beaches of Normandy between 29 July and 4 August.[93].

German forces driven into retreat with notable encounters involving Polish land or airborne troops in Normandy, Belgium and Holland.

In Poland, prior to the city's surrender by Gen. *Komorowski* (1895- 1966) and at the cost of great numbers of dead (approximately 17,000 military and 200,000 civilians perished[94]), *Warsaw* is virtually destroyed by German forces. Polish Home Army is overwhelmed in its final attempt to liberate *Warsaw*, before the arrival of Soviet troops that were pushing units of the German army westwards through Belarus and through Poland.

Bolesław Bierut (1892-1956) appointed as head of the Presidium of the Popular Council.

Creation of a Soviet-sponsored Polish army of 400,000 troops.[95]

Deportation to the Soviet Gulag by Soviet authorities of 50,000 Polish members of the Underground Army.[96]

1945

Polish cities of *Warsaw* and *Kraków,* Hungarian capital (*Budapest*), *Bratislava* in Slovakia and *Vienna* in Austria are all liberated by Allied forces. 2nd Polish Corps liberates *Bologna*.

Hitler commits suicide.

Germany surrenders unconditionally to the Allies.

Potsdam Conference.

U.S. bombing of Hiroshima and Nagasaki in Japan.

Conference at *Yalta* (USSR), Eastern territories in Europe ceded to USSR.

The Polish People's Republic and its 24 million inhabitants[97] formally falls under total Soviet control and becomes part of the Soviet zone of interest, later known as the 'Soviet (or Eastern) Bloc'.

Formation of the Provisional Government of National Unity[98] under Soviet protection.

Creation of the 'United Nations' (Poland is a founding member).

As a result of almost six years of war, although the figures vary[99], Poland lost 6,028,000 of its citizens – the highest ratio of losses to population of any country in Europe; in those areas of Eastern Europe subject to both German and Soviet mass killing alone, the approximate number of those killed numbered fourteen million[100], 11 million of these died in the occupied Polish lands.

1946   Polish armed forces in the West dissolved.[101]

Polish government in **Warsaw** revokes citizenship of Generals *Anders, Maczek, Kopański* and many more high-ranking Polish officers.

Creation of the '*Polish Resettlement Corps*' in Great Britain.

1947   *Bolesław Bierut* becomes President of People's Republic of Poland.

Start of the 'Cold War' between NATO Allies and those of the Eastern Bloc.

Abolishment of the Prussian State.

1948   Stalinist regime forced on people living in Polish People's Republic[102]. Soviet satellite states made to accelerate adoption of its model of social, political and economic control.[103]

UK and USA withdraw recognition of Polish government in exile in London.

1949   Polish Resettlement corps dissolved.[104]

Approximately 500,000[105] Poles settle for a life-in-exile (primarily in Britain, North America, and Australia).

1950   *Tadeusz Reichstein* (1897-1996) becomes Nobel Prize winner for Medicine and Physiology.

1952   Formal Proclamation of the **People's Republic of Poland**.[106]

Position of 'President' abolished, Council of State becomes collective Head of State.

1953   Death of *Stalin*.

1954   Following disclosures about brutality of the regime by *Józef Światło*, Polish Ministry of Security in Poland is abolished.[107]

1955   Signing of the Treaty of *Warsaw* integrating the military forces of the Soviet Bloc[108] (the '*Warsaw Pact*').

1956   Strikes and protests during *Poznań* Uprising.[109]Fighting between workers and Communist Government forces.

Demonstrations in Hungary in sympathy with events in *Poznań* lead to uprising there and invasion of Hungary by Soviet army.

Following the death of *Bolesław Bierut*, *Władysław Gomułka* (1905- 1982) becomes First Secretary of Polish Communist Party.

1958   Death of *Jerzy Dobiecki*.

Since 1958, Poland has seen further tumultuous events, including changes to the country's constitution and to the relationships with neighboring countries in Europe and with the rest of the world. Despite further economic and political hardship that made Poland fall behind other countries in terms of economic development in the West during the years following the Second World War, events took place that might not have been imagined by the thousands of Poles like *Jerzy* – who lived their lives not knowing how long Poland would have to endure a struggle for democratic independence, or to exist under one totalitarian regime or other.

In addition to an evolution in the political thinking in the leadership of the Soviet Union[110], factors such as the birth of the *Solidarność* trade union movement in the shipbuilding yards of *Gdańsk*, and the opposition to the communist regime by the church and by *Karol Wojtiła* (1920-2005) – the Polish Pope – (beatified in May 2011), the world went on to witness a revolution by a restless population in Poland that precipitated the end of the Cold War. The social movements born in Poland that challenged the communist regime, would become a model of dissension for other Eastern European countries.

Following the collapse of communism, the Third Polish Republic formed in 1989 and *The Republic of Poland* was restored as an independent, sovereign state; *Lech Wałęsa* was appointed as the first post-war, democratically elected President in 1990. The crowned eagle was restored as the state emblem of Poland. Germany was unified again in 1991 along with the dissolution of the Warsaw Pact and the collapse of the USSR itself, with full independence being achieved by numerous nation states of the former Soviet Union. The Soviet Army finally began its withdrawal from Poland in 1993, after 45 years of continuous presence.

Poland, Hungary and the Czech Republic became members of NATO in 1999 and Poland joined the European Union in 2004. Today, a Pole – **Donald Tusk** – (former Prime Minister of Poland) is the head of the European Council of Ministers.

Ian von Heintze

APPENDIX TWO

Maps of Poland

1. Extent of the former *'Kingdom of Poland and Lithuania'* prior to Partition in 1772

2. Polish Lands following *Partition* of 1795

3. The *'Duchy of Warsaw'* in 1809

4. The *'Congress Kingdom of Poland'* in 1815

5. The *'Republic of Poland'* in 1918

6. The *'Polish Second Republic'* in 1923

7. The *'Republic of Poland'* in 2016

1. Extent of the former 'Kingdom of Poland and Lithuania' prior to the first Partition in **1772** (against background of modern-day states of Europe)

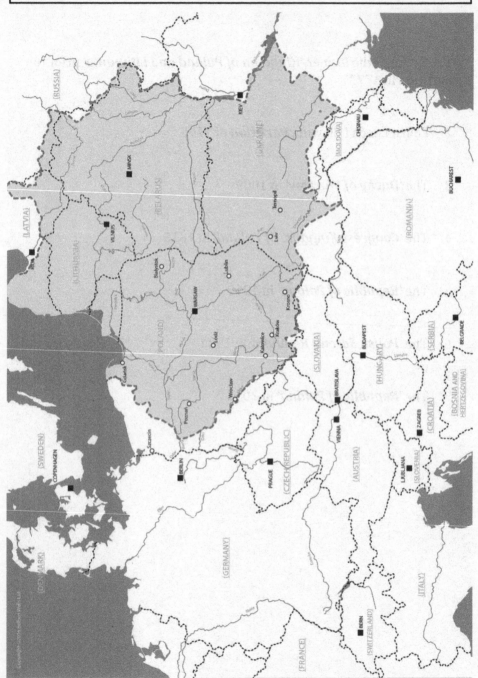

2. Polish Lands following partition in **1795**
(against background of modern-day states of Europe)

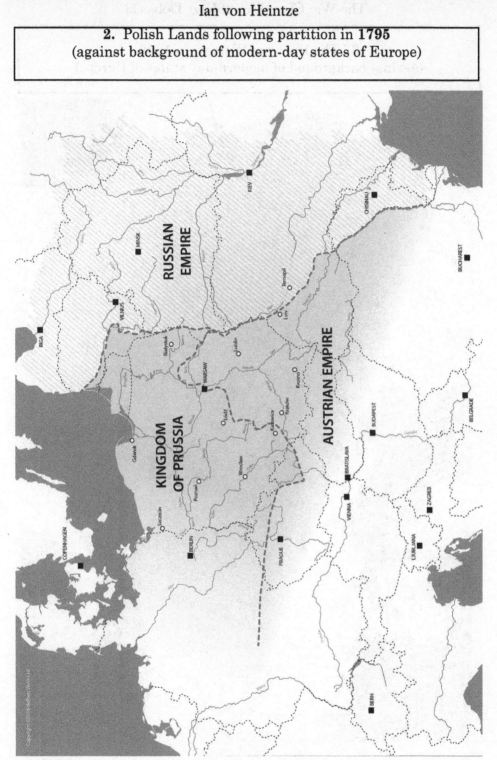

3. The Duchy of Warsaw in **1809**
(against background of modern-day states of Europe)

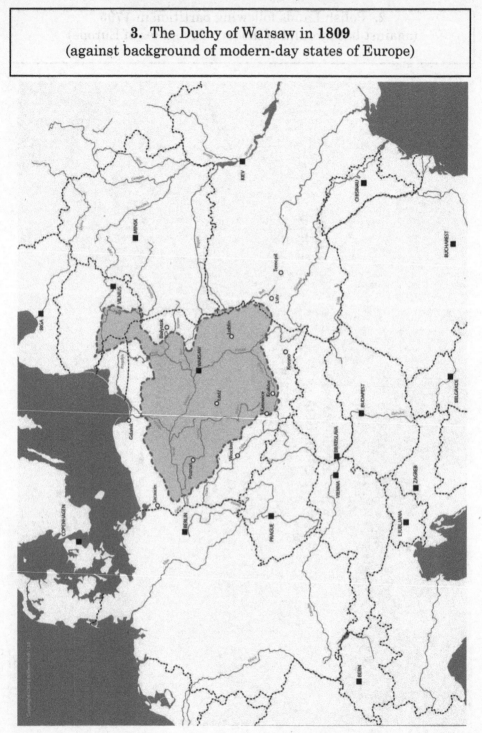

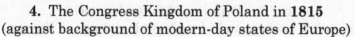

4. The Congress Kingdom of Poland in 1815
(against background of modern-day states of Europe)

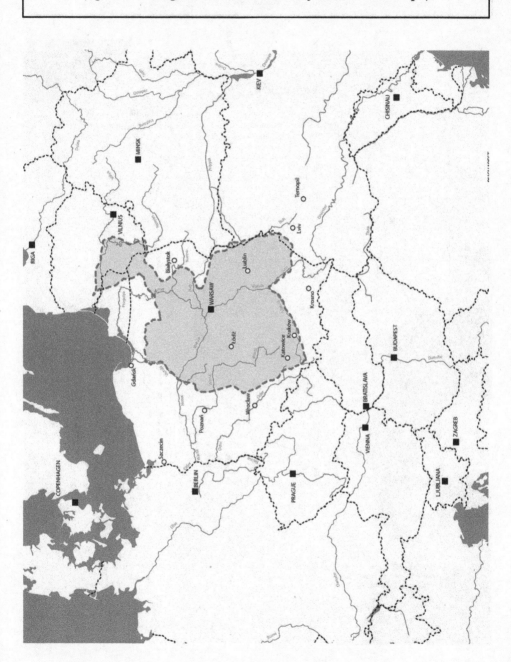

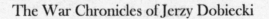

5. The Republic of Poland in **1918**
(against background of modern-day states of Europe)

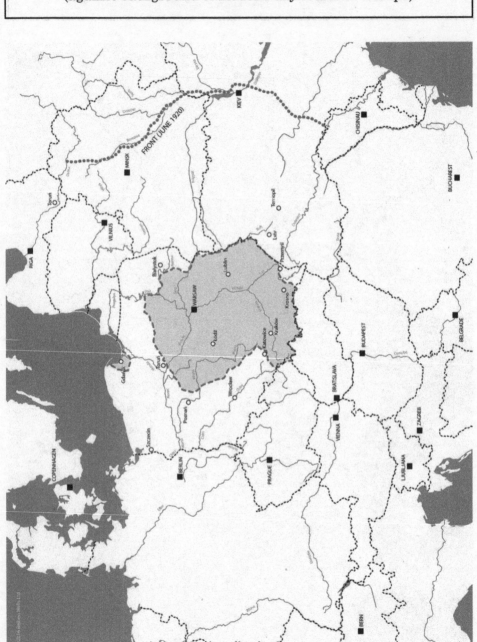

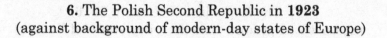

6. The Polish Second Republic in **1923**
(against background of modern-day states of Europe)

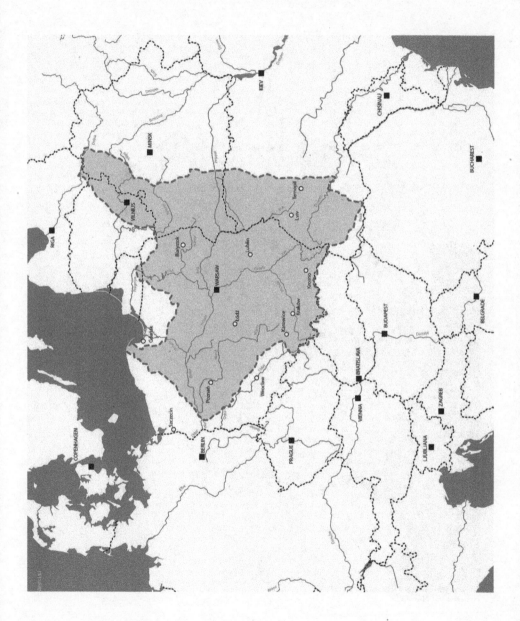

7. The Republic of Poland in **2016**
(against background of modern-day states of Europe)

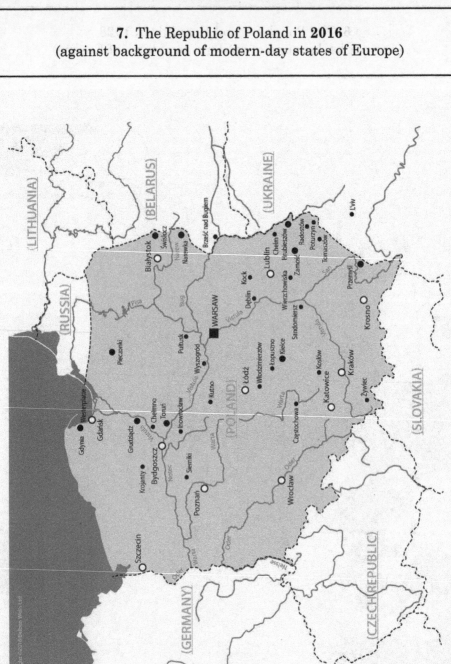

Ian von Heintze

APPENDIX THREE

Dobiecki Family Lineage
Image of Family Crest © Adam Boniecki
Page Design © Belben Wells (UK) Ltd

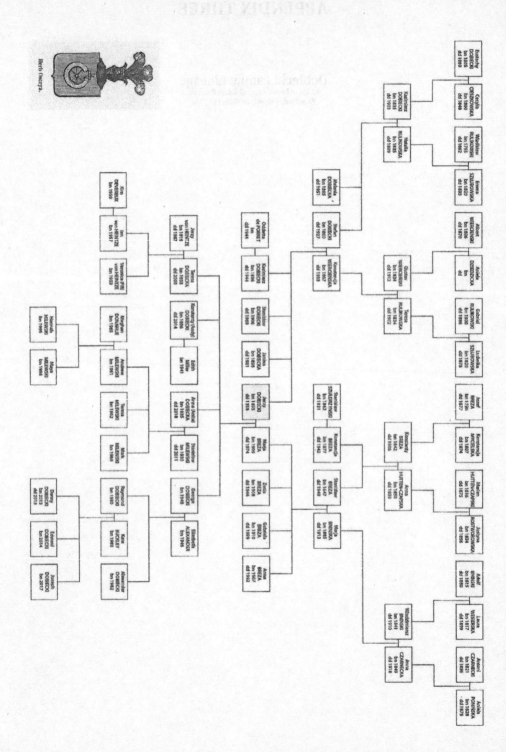

Herb Ostrya.

Ian von Heintze

APPENDIX FOUR

A) The Polish Army from 1919 to 1920
B) The main branches of service in the Polish Army in 1920
C) Allocation of Armies to Fronts (from March 1920 onwards)

Extracts reproduced by kind permission of OSPREY publishing
© 2014 N. Thomas PhD. 'Armies of the Russo-Polish War 1919-21'

APPENDIX FOUR
The Polish Army from 1919 to 1920

Extracts reproduced by kind permission of OSPREY publishing © 2014 N. Thomas PhD. 'Armies of the Russo-Polish War 1919-21'

Following the end of the Great War, Poland assembled a new army of its own and was almost immediately engaged in six wars with neighboring states. Between 1918 and 1921, there were a number of changes made to the structure of Poland's army that was not only fighting battles on several Fronts but had also to modify its strategies as the more serious threat posed by Germany diminished and the menace of the spread of communism from Russia increased. This led to an extremely complicated and constantly evolving picture of the Army's structure, leadership and deployment, particularly during this period of 1919 to 1921. In early 1919, although estimates vary, Poland had some 110,000 serving soldiers and this figure grew to around 600,000 men over the following years. As the war with Russia developed, there was no clear-cut confrontation between the armies involved. Consequently, it is difficult to set out an 'Order of Battle' that portrays - in the conventional way, the disposition of Polish forces during the wars of this period. Later in 1939, the task of listing Poland's forces and how the various elements that were about to engage in the Second World War were organized, became much clearer (see Appendix 3).

Key Dates

3 June 1918	Allied Governments recognize the principle of Polish Independence
30 October 1918	Creation of the first independent Polish military units
11 November 1918	Armistice on Western Front ending the Great War
11 November 1918	Formation of the Polish Army, Józef Piłsudski appointed Commander-in-Chief
14 February 1919	Start of the first hostilities between Poland and Russia in what was to become the **Russo/Polish War**
26 February 1919	Introduction of the Army Law, reorganization of the Polish army
7 March 1919	Introduction of conscription
24 July 1919	Formation of the '4th Greater Poland Lancers Regiment' (also called the 'Vistula Lancers Regiment')
5 March 1920	4th G. P. Lancers officially re-designated the '18th Polish Pomeranian Lancers Regiment'
23 March 1920	Polish land Army re-grouped into 8 'Armies'
29 May 1920	18th Polish Pomeranian Lancers deployed to the Northern Front during the Russo-Polish War

Ian von Heintze

The main branches of service in the Polish Army in 1920

Extracts reproduced by kind permission of OSPREY publishing © 2014 N. Thomas PhD. 'Armies of the Russo-Polish War 1919-21'

GENERAL STAFF
CAVALRY & INFANTRY:

Divisions
Brigades
Regiments
Battalions
Squadrons/Companies
Platoons & Sections

ARTILLERY
ARMOUR
AIR SERVICE
ENGINEERS
SIGNALS
MILITARY POLICE
TRANSPORT SERVICE
MEDICAL SERVICE
BORDER GUARD

Groupings of the Polish Army (1920)

FIRST ARMY
SECOND ARMY
THIRD ARMY
FOURTH ARMY
FIFTH ARMY
SIXTH ARMY
SEVENTH ARMY
RESERVE ARMY

Rank Structure of the Army/ Cavalry (1920)

Marshal
General of the Army
General of Division
Brigadier General
Colonel
Major
Captain (*Rotmistrz*)
Lieutenant
Second Lieutenant
Officer Cadet

Warrant Officer/Staff Sgt/Sergeant/ Lance-Sergeant/Corporal/Lance Corporal

Private/Trooper/Lancer/ Rifleman/Sapper/Gunner

Allocation of Armies to Fronts (from March 1920 onwards)

Extracts reproduced by kind permission of OSPREY publishing © 2014 N. Thomas PhD. 'Armies of the Russo-Polish War 1919-21'

NORTHERN FRONT

FIRST ARMY (17 MAY – 23 AUG 1920)
SECOND ARMY (6 – 16 AUG 1920)
FOURTH ARMY (*Gen. Skierski*) (17 MAY - 8 AUG 1920)
-11th Infantry Division
-16th Pomeranian Division
-14th Greater Poland Infantry Division
-15th Greater Poland Infantry Division
        18th Polish Pomeranian Lancers- 29 MAY 1920, attached to 1st Cavalry
                            Brigade, 'Dźwina Operating Group' of
                            Gen. *SOSNKOWSKI*
                            - 22ND SEPT 1920, attached to Operating
                            Group of Gen. *JUNG*
SEVENTH ARMY (17 MAY-15 JUNE 1920)
RESERVE ARMY (25 MAY-15 JUNE 1920)

CENTRAL FRONT

SECOND ARMY (19 JUNE - 6 AUG 1920)
THIRD ARMY (28 MAY- 23 AUG 1920)
FOURTH ARMY (4 - 23 AUG 1920)
SIXTH ARMY (28 MAY-10 AUG 1920)

SOUTHERN FRONT

SIXTH ARMY (10 AUG - 6 SEPT)
UKRAINIAN ARMY (10 AUG - 6 SEPT)

Ian von Heintze

APPENDIX FIVE

Polish Army Order of Battle, 1 September 1939

APPENDIX FIVE

Polish Army Order of Battle, 1st September 1939

Extracts reproduced by kind permission of OSPREY publishing © 2009,
'Poland 1939 The birth of Blitzkrieg'

Army Pomorze — Gen Div W. Bortkowski

9th Infantry Division	Col J. Werobej
15th Infantry Division	Brig Gen Z. Przyjałkowski
27th Infantry Division	Brig Gen J. Drapella
Group Wschod	Brig Gen M. Bołtuć
4th Infantry Division	Col T. Lubicz-Niezabitowski
16th Infantry Division	Col S. Świtalski
Group Czersk	Brig Gen Grzmot-Skotnicki
Pomeranian Cavalry Brigade	Col A. Zakrzewski

**Incl. (18th Polish Pomeranian Lancers) (Col K. Mastalerz)

Army Modlin — Brig Gen E. Krukowicz-Przedrzymirski

8th Infantry Division	Col T.W. Furgalski
20th Infantry Division	Col W.A. Lawin-Liszka
Nowogrodzka Cavalry Brigade	Brig Gen W. Anders
Mazowiecka Cavalry Brigade	Col J. Karcz
Group Wyszków	Brig Gen W. Kowalski
1st Legion Infantry Division	Brig Gen W. Kowalski
41st Reserve Infantry Division	Brig Gen W. Piekarski
Sp. Ops Group Narew	Brig Gen C. Młot-Fijałowski
18th Infantry Division	Col S. Kossecki
33rd Reserve Infantry Division	Col T. Kalina-Zieleniewski
Podolska Cavalry Brigade	Big Gen L. Kmicic-Skrzyński
Suwalska Cavalry Brigade	Brig Gen Z. Podhorski

Army Poznań — Gen Div T. Kutrzeba

14th Infantry Division	Brig Gen F. Wład
17th Greater Poland Infantry Division	Col M. Mozdyniewicz
25th Infantry Division	Brig Gen F. Alter
26th Infantry Division	Col A. Brzechwa-Ajdukiewicz
Greater Poland Cavalry Brigade	Brig Gen R. Abraham
Podolska Cavalry Brigade	Col L. Strzelecki

Army Łódź Gen Div J. Rommel

2nd Legion Infantry Division	Col E. Dojan-Surówka
10th Infantry Division	Brig Gen F. Dindorf-Ankowicz
28th Infantry Division	Brig Gen Bończa-Uzdowski
Kresowa Cavalry Brigade	Col S. Kulesza
Group Piotrków	Brig Gen W. Thommée
30th Infantry Division	Brig Gen L. Cehak
Wołyńska Cavalry Brigade	Col J. Filipowicz

Army Prusy Gen Div S. Dąb-Biernacki

13th Infantry Division	Col W. Zubosz-Kaliński
29th Infantry Division	Col. I. Ozierewicz
Cavalry Operational Group	Brig Gen R. Dreszer
19th Infantry Division	Brig Gen Skwarczyński
Wołyńska Cavalry Brigade	Col K. Drucki-Lubecki
Skwarczynski Operational Group	Brig Gen Skwarczyński
3rd Legion Infantry Division	Col M. Turkowski
12th Infantry Division	Brig Gen G. Paszkiewicz
36th Reserve Infantry Division	Col B. Ostrowski

Army Kraków Brig Gen A. Szylling

6th Infantry Division	Brig Gen B. Mond
7th Infantry Division	Brig Gen I. Gąsiorowski
10th Mechanized Brigade	Col S. Maczek
Krakowska Cavalry Brigade	Brig Gen Z. Piasecki
Group Śląsk	Brig Gen J. Jagmin-Sadowski
23rd Górnośląska Infantry Division	Col W. Powierza
55th Reserve Infantry Division	Col S. Kolabiński
Group Bielsko	Brig Gen M. Boruta-Spiechowicz
1st Mounted Brigade	Col E. Żongołłowicz
21st Mountain Infantry Division	Brig Gen J. Kustroń

Army Karpaty Gen Div K. Fabrycy

2nd Mountain Brigade	Col A. Stawarz
3rd Mountain Brigade	Col J. Kotowicz

FOOTNOTES

SOME HELP WITH PRONUNCIATION OF POLISH WORDS

1.Corbridge-Patkaniowska M. *POLISH – A simplified course for beginners*, John Murray Press, a division of Hodder & Stoughton, 1982, pp. 1-7

PREFACE

1.Kłopotowski M. & Dobiecki J. *Zarys historji wojennej 18-go Pułku Ułanów Pomorskich*, Warsaw, 1929.
Accessed via: Polish Academy of Sciences, Kórnik Library, Kórnik, Poland
Digital Library of Greater Poland
http://www.wbc.poznan.pl/publication/31545
2. Davies N. *White Eagle, Red Star*, Pimlico, 2003, p. xv
3. Davies N. *God's Playground – A History of Poland, volume II*, Columbia University Press, 1982, p. 398
4. Dobiecki J. Rtm. *Personal archived Notes*, Paris 1940
      Accessed via: Polish Institute and Sikorski Museum, London,
      ref: archives/documents/B.I.1-130/file B.I.28g/document 10
5. Kochański H. *The Eagle Unbowed – Poland and the Poles in the Second World War*, Penguin Books, 2013, p. 86
6. Kwiecień M. *Wśród potępieńczych swarów. Prawne aspekty rozliczeń politycznych wśród uchodźstwa polskiego we Francji i wielkiej Brytanii 1939-1943,* Księgarnia Akademicka, Kraków, 2013 (Summary in English) Accessed via: Library of Congress, Washington USA
7. Zamoyski A. *The Polish Way*, John Murray Publishers Ltd, 1987, p. 257
8. Zamoyski A. Ibid. p. 266 and Lukowski J. & Zawadzki H. *A Concise History of Poland* (Second Edition), Cambridge University Press, 2007, p. 136
9. Zamoyski A. op. cit. p. 267

POLISH CAVALRY LEGEND

1. Zamoyski A.op. cit., p. 155-156

CHAPTER 1

1. Details of Wiercieński family ancestry (in Polish) accessed via http://www.otostrona.pl/wiercinski/index.php?p=1_36_X

CHAPTER 3

1. Lukowski J. &. Zawadzki H. *A Concise History of Poland*, Second Edition, Cambridge University Press, 2007, p. 222
2. Zamoyski A.op. cit., p. 347
3. Davies N.op. cit., p. 23
4. Ibid. p. 23
5. Thomas N. *Armies of the Russo-Polish War 1919-21*, Osprey Publishing, 2014, p. 4

CHAPTER 4

1. Kłopotowski M. & Dobiecki J. *Zarys historji wojennej 18-go Pułku Ułanów Pomorskich*, Warsaw, 1929. Accessed via: Polish Academy of Sciences, Kórnik Library, Kórnik, Poland http://www.wbc.poznan.pl/publication/31545. Sławomir Ziętarski (of the 18th Polish Pomeranian Lancers Regimental Volunteer Association, Poland) *Historia 18 Pułku Ułanów Pomorskich* Accessed vide: www.18u.pl
2. *Słownik wojskowy angielsko – polski, Polish – English Military Dictionary*, Centralna Komisja Regulaminowa, Wielka Brytania, 1943, p.163

CHAPTER 8

1. Zaloga S. *The Polish Army 1939-1945,* Osprey, 1982, p. 9
2. Sławomir Ziętarski (of the 18th Polish Pomeranian Lancers Regimental Volunteer Association) *Historia 18 Pułku Ułanów Pomorskich* Accessed vide: www.18u.pl
3. *Battles of World War II Poland 1939 The birth of Blitzkrieg,* Osprey Publishing, 2009, UK, p. 43
4. Dobiecki J. Rtm. *Personal archived Notes,* Paris 1940 Accessed via: Polish Institute and Sikorski Museum, London, ref: archives/documents/B.I.1-130/file B.I.28g/document 10
5. Dr Dianna Henderson, *The Lion and the Eagle*, Cualann Press, October 2001, p. 96/7
6. *Research by Robert M. Ostrycharz* Copyright material Accessed via:
http://www.polishforcesinbritain.info/Locations.htm
http://www.polishforcesinbritain.info/PolonicaEastendHouse.htm
http://www.ostrycharz.free-online.co.uk/PolonicainScotland.html#Post_War_Polonica

CHAPTER 9

1. Kochanski H. op. cit., Penguin Books 2013 p.525
2. Extract from *HANSARD* (UK Parliamentary Archives)
   Copy accessed vide: www.parliament.uk/archives
  Ref: http://hansard.millbanksystems.com/commons/1946/mar/20/polish-armed-forces-government-policy
Right of use: Parliamentary information, licensed under the Open Parliament License v3.0.
https://www.parliament.uk/site-information/copyright-parliament/open-parliament-licence/
3. Henderson D.op. cit., p. 143
4. Ibid. p. 66

APPENDIX ONE

1. Zamoyski A.op. cit., p. 253
2. Prażmowska A. *A History of Poland*, Second Edition, Palgrave Macmillan, 2011, p. 130
3. Pogonowski I. *POLAND – An Illustrated History*, Hippocrene Books, 2000, p. 146
4. Prażmowska A. op. cit. p. 133
5. Zamoyski A. op. cit. p. 260
6. Prażmowska A. op. cit. p. 134
7. Zamoyski A. op. cit. p. 259
8. Davies N. op. cit., p. 295
9. Ibid. p. 141
10. Lukowski J. & Zawadzki H. *A Concise History of Poland* (Second Edition), Cambridge University Press, 2007, p. 143
11. Ibid. p.141
12. Ibid. p.143
13. Davies N. op. cit. p. 269
14. Pogonowski I. op. cit. p. 151
15. Zamoyski A. op. cit. p. 264
16. Lukowski/Zawadzki, op. cit. p. 155
17. Ibid. p. 156
18. Davies N. op. cit. p.311
19. Ibid. p. 231
20. Lukowski/Zawadzki, op. cit. p. 155
21. Zamoyski A. op. cit. p. 310
22. Davies N. op. cit. p. 311
23. Lukowski/Zawadzki, op. cit. p. 153
24. Pogonowski I. op. cit. p. 159
25. Lukowski/Zawadzki, op. cit. p.161

26. Davies N. op. cit. p. 324
27. Prażmowska A. op. cit. p.140
28. Ibid. p. 141
29. Lukowski/Zawadzki, op. cit. p. 163
30. Pogonowski I. op. cit. p. 162
31. Davies N. op. cit. p. 331
32. *Gazeta Cukrownicza* (Sugar Industry Magazine) issue 3/2011, Article in Polish by Bogdan Mardofel, accessed vide:
                http://www.sigma-not.pl
                    http://greatcomposers.nifc.pl/en/chopin/catalogs/places/105
33. Lukowski/Zawadzki, op. cit. p. 165
34. Davies N. op. cit. p. 333
35. Zamoyski A. op. cit. p.276
36. Lukowski/Zawadzki, op. cit. p. xxvii
37. Zamoyski A. op. cit. p. 306
38. Lukowski/Zawadzki, op. cit. p. 168
39. Davies N. op. cit. p. 163/4
40. Lukowski/Zawadzki, op. cit. p. 173
41. Prażmowska A. op. cit. p. 147
42. Ibid. p. 148
43. Zamoyski A. op. cit. p. 284
44. Davies N. op. cit. p. 364
45. Lukowski/Zawadzki, op. cit. p. xxvii
46. Prażmowska A. op. cit. p. 154
47. Ibid. p. 148
48. Personal, unpublished correspondence of Jerzy Dobiecki
49. Davies N. op. cit. p. 369
50. Lukowski/Zawadzki, op. cit. p. 208
51. Pogonowski I. op. cit. p. 192
52. Zamoyski A. op. cit. p. 333
53. Davies N. op. cit. p. 378
54. Strachan H. *The First World War*, Simon and Schuster, 2014, p. 42
55. McGilvray E. *The Black Devil's March*, Helion & Co Ltd, 2010, p. 2
56. Lukowski/Zawadzki, op. cit. p. 218
57. Ibid. p. 217
58. Davies N. op. cit. p. 381
59. Ibid. p. xxv
60. Prażmowska A. op. cit. p. 164
61. Davies N. op. cit., p. 20
62. Strachan H. op. cit. p. xviii
63. Zamoyski A. op. cit. p. 333
64. Lukowski/Zawadzki, op. cit. p. 229

65. Prażmowska A. op. cit. p. 169
66. Lukowski/Zawadzki, op. cit. p. 232
67. Ibid. p. xxix
68. Ibid. p. 244
69. Ibid. p. xxix
70. Ibid. p. xxix
71. Ibid. p. 253
72. Pogonowski I. op. cit. p. 212
73. Davies N. op. cit., p. 435
74. Kochański H. op. cit., p. 63
75. Pogonowski I. op. cit. p. 216
76. Prażmowska A. op. cit. p. 179 and Jarzembowski J. *Armored Hussars*, Helion & Co, 2014, p. vii
77. Pogonowski I. op. cit. p. 216
78. Lukowski/Zawadzki, op. cit. p. xxx
79. Jarzembowski J. op. cit. p. viii
80. Davies N. op. cit. p. 285
81. Lukowski/Zawadzki, op. cit. p. 263
82. McGilvray E. op. cit. p. 6
83. Olson L. & Cloud C. *A Question of Honor,* New York, 2003, p. 109
84. Lukowski/Zawadzki, op. cit. p. 264
85. Davies N. op. cit. p. 452
86. Lukowski/Zawadzki, op. cit. p. 263
87. Ibid. p. 256
88. Prażmowska A. op. cit. p. 184
89 Lukowski/Zawadzki, op. cit. p. 267
90. Ibid. p. 268
91. Davies N. op. cit. p. xxvi
92. McGilvray E. op. cit. p.8
93. J. Jarzembowski, op. cit. p. viii
94. Lukowski/Zawadzki, op. cit. p. 272
95. Ibid. p. 272
96. Ibid. p. 275
97. Ibid. p. 281
98. Davies N. op. cit. p. xxvii
99. Ibid. p. 463
100. Lukas R.C. *Forgotten Holocaust*, Hippocrene Books, 1997, pp. 38-9, and Snyder T. *Blood Lands*, Vintage Books, 2015, p. 409
101. Lukowski/Zawadzki, op. cit. p. xxxi
102. Ibid. p. xxxi
103. Ibid. p. 286
104. Jarzembowski J. op. cit. p. ix
105. Lukowski/Zawadzki, op. cit. p. 280

106. Ibid. p. xxxi
107. Davies N op. cit. p. 582
108. Lukowski/Zawadzki, op. cit. p. xxxi
109. Ibid. p. 295
110. A. Kemp-Welch *Poland under Communism*, Cambridge University Press, 2008, p. 361

REFERENCES

Boniecki, Adam. *Herbarz Polski* - Cześć I, Tom IV. Warszawa, 1902

Centralna Komisja Regulaminowa. *Słownik Wojskowy Polish-English Military Dictionary*, Printed in Edinburgh, 1943

Cornish, Nik. *The Russian Army1914-18*. Cambridge: Osprey Publishing, 2001.

Davies, Norman. *God's Playground: A History of Poland Volume II, 1795 to Present*. New York: Columbia University Press, 1982

Davies, Norman. *White Eagle, Red Star: The Polish-Soviet War 1919-1920*. London: Pimlico, 2001.

Gilbert, Martin. *The Second World War*. London: Fontana/Collins, 1990.

Hayward, Brigadier P. *Jane's Dictionary of Military Terms*. London: MacDonald & Co, 1975.

Henderson, D. *The Lion and the Eagle*. London: Cualann Press, 2001

Howard, Michael. *The First World War: A Very Short Introduction*. Oxford: Oxford University Press 2002.

Kemp-Welch, A. *Poland under Communism*. Cambridge: Cambridge University Press, 2008

Kobak, Annette. *Joe's War (My Father decoded)*. New York: Vintage Books (Random House Publishing) 2004.

Kochański, Halik. *The Eagle Unbowed*. London: Penguin Books, 2013.

Kłopotowski, M & Dobiecki, J. *Zarys historji wojennej 18-go Pułku Ułanów Pomorskich*. Warsaw, 1929. Available through: Polish Academy of Sciences, Kornik Library, Kornik, Poland.
 http://www.wbc.poznan.pl/publication/31545

Kwiecień, M. *Wśród potępieńczych swarów. Prawne aspekty rozliczeń politycznych wśród uchodźstwa polskiego we Francji i wielkiej Brytanii 1939-1943*. Krakow: Księgarnia Akademicka, 2013. (Summary in English) Available through: Library of Congress, Washington, USA

Jarzembowski, Janusz. *Armored Hussars*. London: Helion & Co, 2014.

Lukowski, Jerzy and Zawadzki, Hubert. *A Concise History of Poland* (Second Edition). Cambridge: Cambridge University Press, 2007.

Lukas, Richard. *Forgotten Holocaust: The Poles under German Occupation 1939-1944*. New York: Hippocrene Books, Revised Edition, 1997

McGilvray, Evan. *The Black Devil's March: The 1st Polish Armored Division 1939-45*. London: Helion & Co, 2010.

Nobility of The Polish Commonwealth Polish Nobility Association Foundation Maryland, 1983.

Olson, Lynne & Cloud, Stanley. *A Question of Honour The Kościuszko Squadron*. New York: Alfred Knopf Publishers, 2003.

Ostrowski, Mark. *To Return to Poland or not to Return (The Dilemma facing the Polish Armed Forces at the end of the second world war)*. London: School of Slavonic & European Studies University of London
http://discovery.ucl.ac.uk/1349014/1/DX194948.pdf

Piotrowski, Tadeusz (ed). *The Polish Deportees of World War II*. London: Mc Farland & Co, 2004.

Pogonowski, Cyprian. *Poland - An Illustrated History*. New York: Iwo Hippocrene Books, 2000.

Prażmowska, Anita. *A History of Poland*. Second Edition. London: Palgrave/ Macmillan, 2011

Rospond, Vincent. *The Polish Army in 1939*. Point Pleasant: Winged Hussar Publishing, 2016.

Snyder, Timothy. *Blood Lands: Europe between Hitler and Stalin*. London: Vintage Books, 2015.

Strachan, Hew. *The First World War*. London: Simon & Schuster, 2014.

Thomas, Nigel, Phd. *Armies of the Russo-Polish War 1919-21*. London: Osprey Publishing, 2014.

Ian von Heintze

Zaloga, Steve. *Battles of World War II: Poland 1939 The Birth of Blitzkrieg*. Cambridge: Osprey Publishing, 2009.

Zaloga, Steven. *The Polish Army 1939-45*. Oxford: Osprey Publishing, 2008.

Zamoyski, Adam. *The Polish Way*. London: John Murray, 1987.

Zamoyski, Adam. *Warsaw 1920*. London: William Collins, 2014.

Ziętarski, Sławomir. *Historia 18 Pułku Ułanów Pomorskich* (18th Polish Pomeranian Lancers Regimental Volunteer Association). Poland. www.18u.pl

ACKNOWLEDGEMENTS

I owe a great debt of gratitude to my wife, Kim. Had it not been for her enthusiasm, wise, humorous and always inspired suggestions – that came at precisely the right moment, I very much doubt that this project would have come together in the way that it has. As always, I thank her for her love, genuine interest and unwavering support.

I would like to extend special thanks to Joanna Machnica, Member of the Chartered Institute of Linguists, for translating the Polish texts upon which sections of this book are based. Her professional help and advice about the documents that have been drawn from archives in England and in Poland, together with her assistance in the many communications between myself and the individuals or institutions in Poland, have made this book possible.

Both Dr Andrzej Suchcitz, Keeper of Archives of the Polish Institute and Sikorski Museum in London, and Professor Tomasz Jasiński, Director of the Kórnik Library of the Polish Academy of Sciences in Poland, were kind enough to give me permission to have the chronicles written in Polish by my grandfather and archived with those institutions, translated into English and used in this book. Details of how these archived works may be accessed are shown in the Footnotes section. I am equally grateful to Osprey Publishing for giving me permission to reproduce and include in appendices to this book, details of Poland's military structure in 1920 and the Order of Battle of the Polish Army later in 1939, at the outbreak of the Second World War.

My thanks go to Sławomir Ziętarski of the 18th Polish Pomeranian Lancers' Regimental Volunteer Association in Poland, for his help and kind permission to have translated into English, a historical piece written by him about my grandfather's regiment during its short twenty-year history between 1919 and 1939. Mr. Ziętarski's article can be found, in Polish, on the Association's website (www.18u.pl). I am also grateful for the help of Regina Frąckowiak, a Reference Specialist at the European Division of the Library of Congress, Washington D.C. in The United States, to the staff at the UK Ministry of Defense Polish War records office, and to Liam Cloud and Jane Rockett for assisting with the numerous printing tasks associated with production of the draft manuscript. Geoff Belben and Graham Wells were instrumental in drawing most of the maps that appear in this book including the family tree, and I thank them for their skill and advice throughout the process. Thank you to Drew and Joy Yapp for their help with the production of the images that appear on the front cover and elsewhere in the book.

Thank you also to George Dobiecki, Edith Dobiecki, Anita Milewski and to Fifi von Heintze for enabling me to lay my hands on all the family documents and photographs and to Kim, Joanna, George and Mark Milewski for assisting me greatly with the initial proof-reading of the draft manuscript.

Finally, I am so grateful to my publisher, Vincent Rospond of Pike and Powder Publishing LLC, for his endorsement of my work and for agreeing to take this project on. His advice and wise counsel are much appreciated.

THE AUTHOR

Ian von Heintze was born in England and is the son of Polish parents who fled Poland to Britain either during or immediately after the Second World War. His father, detained in 1940 in Warsaw by means of the notorious Nazi 'łapanka' (random street arrests), was among those Polish political prisoners able to remarkably achieve release from the camp at Auschwitz towards the end of 1940.

A language graduate and former Member of the Chartered Institute of Linguists, Ian retired in 2001 following a career in London's Metropolitan Police, attaining the rank of Inspector attached to Scotland Yard's Specialist Operations Directorate.

He maintains his keen interest in Polish history today and in 2009 published the story about the lives of his Polish family in his book 'To Remain on File'.

INDEX

The War Chronicles of Jerzy Dobiecki

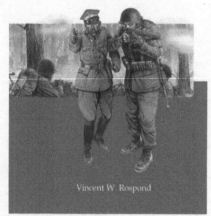

The Polish Army
in 1939

Vincent W. Rospond

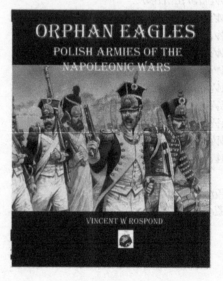

ORPHAN EAGLES
POLISH ARMIES OF THE
NAPOLEONIC WARS

VINCENT W ROSPOND